Surviving
the Sand

Five years after the beginning of the adventure. Pictured left to right: Frank, Dad, Mom, Emma, Helen, and (in front) Hazel on the farm. The hills in the background are the Blue Mountains, about 60 miles away.

Surviving the Sand

MY FAMILY'S STRUGGLE TO FARM THE PASCO DESERT

HELEN LINGSCHEIT HEAVIRLAND

ILLUSTRATIONS BY CARYN LAWTON

BASALT BOOKS
PULLMAN, WA

BASALT BOOKS

Basalt Books
PO Box 645910
Pullman, WA 99164

Library of Congress Cataloging-in-Publication Data
Library of Congress Cataloging-in-Publication Data

Names: Heavirland, Helen, 1946- author.
Title: Surviving the sand : my family's struggle to farm the Pasco Desert /
   Helen Lingscheit Heavirland.
Description: Pullman, WA : Basalt Books, [2022] | Audience: Ages 10 and up
Identifiers: LCCN 2022033442 | ISBN 9781638640042 (paperback)
Subjects: LCSH: Heavirland, Helen, 1946---Childhood and youth--Juvenile
   literature. | Columbia Basin Project (U.S.)--Juvenile literature. |
   Girls--Washington (State)--Pasco--Biography--Juvenile literature. | Farm
   life--Washington (State)--Pasco--Juvenile literature. | Pasco
   (Wash.)--Biography--Juvenile literature.
Classification: LCC F897.F8 H43 2022 | DDC 979.7/33092
   [B]--dc23/eng/20220831
LC record available at https://lccn.loc.gov/2022033442

Basalt Books is an imprint of Washington State University Press.

The Washington State University Pullman campus is located on the homelands of the Niimíipuu (Nez Perce) Tribe and the Palus people. We acknowledge their presence here since time immemorial and recognize their continuing connection to the land, to the water, and to their ancestors. WSU Press is committed to publishing works that foster a deeper understanding of the Pacific Northwest and the contributions of its Native peoples.

Cover art by Caryn Lawton
Cover design by Jeffry E. Hipp

Contents

1959

1959 and Beyond

Dedication

To Mom
who sacrificed from her heart
for someone else's dream
and from whom, in spite of heartbreaking circumstances,
not one of us kids
ever heard a word of complaint.

To Dad
who dreamed,
had his dreams blown away . . . repeatedly,
but kept going until they grew into reality.

To my brother and sisters
who survived the lean years,
worked like troopers to help things change,
and became both tough and compassionate.

To the other Columbia Basin pioneers
whose footprints in the sand blew to their neighbors,
who, from whatever clime they came,
learned to love the sky so wide it had no end
and the land so level you could see for miles,
who gave all they were
and did it again every time the windblown sand
destroyed their latest hope,
who risked everything on unproven acreage
and proved their own grit was stronger than sand,
who transformed miles and miles of desert
into fields that feed the world.

Introduction

One spring day my husband and I drove from Montana to visit Mom and Dad on the eastern Washington farm where I'd grown up. The wind gusts made it hard to keep our car on the road. Blowing sand made it difficult to see. Shortly after we'd fought the wind and dust through that area, Highway 395 south of Ritzville was closed due to low visibility—a not uncommon occurrence.

When we crawled out of the car at the farm, the wind nearly blew us to the farmhouse. We'd been inside only a few minutes when I noticed corn seeds a couple inches apart in three rows the length of the coffee table. Puzzled, I asked, "What's with the corn on the coffee table?"

Mom got an impish grin. "I dusted three times this afternoon," she said in mock seriousness. "The sand just keeps blowing in. Decided I may as well plant corn!"

We all laughed, but the wind, the sand, and the twinkle in Mom's eyes, triggered a flood of memories for me.

The events recorded in *Surviving the Sand* are real—all too real! I have researched to assure accuracy of the facts that memory might have colored. The people are real. Where I thought it wise, I have changed the names of a few, but they are real people. Dialogue? My brother, sisters, and I simply can't remember word-for-word all the conversations of our youth. I have re-created dialogue to fit memory and the personality of different family members. (To protect myself from friendly family insurrection, my siblings have read, helped edit, and approved drafts of the book you hold.)

Oh, the memories. In the early 1950s, much of the Columbia Basin was still desert—think sagebrush, sandburs, horned toads, scorpions, rattlesnakes. Grateful for irrigation, new settlers broke sod. At first many lived in shacks or tents while they looked forward to bountiful harvests to supply money for building adequate housing. These farmers arrived with varying assets, varying motivation, and varying knowledge of farming. They soon discovered that none of the roads were named Easy Street.

Surviving the Sand gives a peek at trying to tame desert. But it's more than one family's memoir. It's the near-story of many a farm family in the arid American West. It is grassroots history. *Surviving the Sand* reveals pioneer spirit reborn in the 1950's.

Why did families even consider trying to farm desert? Why was it even possible?

For a brief history that gives deeper context to the hard-scrabble and heartwarming story that follows, go to "Historical Setting," page 249.

CHAPTER 1

Home?

D ad's eyes danced. His grin held happiness . . . hope. "We're home!" he announced.

Mom stared out the pickup window. Silent. Lifeless.

Scattered tufts of skinny grass and small grayish-green bushes surrounded us. The land lay flat in every direction as far as I could see.

Sixteen-year-old Emma looked front and back. She gazed side to side. Brow furrows deepened. Finally, her dumbfounded question exploded the silence. "Where's the house?"

"There!" thirteen-year-old Frank declared with pride and smug wisdom. He pointed to a shed.

I gawked. It wasn't even big enough to hold our beds. This didn't look like home to me!

The only home I'd known was a comfortable white house with red geraniums in window boxes. Home sat in the mountains of Oregon's Coast Range. Home was surrounded by fragrant fir and pine forests full of colorful wildflowers. From our backyard we could see a waterfall cascade over a sheer cliff. Home was beautiful.

What was happening? How could Dad call *this* home?

It had been only a few weeks since Dad had disrupted the peace and beauty that had been our home in western Oregon for all of my seven years. That evening, supper had been a normal meal with family banter . . . until Dad dropped his bombshell. "I've got some news!" he proclaimed.

Frank quit teasing Emma. Her evil-eye glare at him melted. We all looked at Dad.

"We're going to move," he proclaimed. His voice had a lilt, like when he announced an upcoming family picnic or a trip over the mountains to the beach.

Move? I wondered. *We* were *all moving—spooning soup to our mouths—until he stopped us.*

"Yes!" Dad's eyes sparkled. "You've heard me tell story after story about growing up on my grandpa and grandma's farm in southern Idaho. I've wanted to farm ever since. Through the years we've made a living logging and running a sawmill. But, this close to the Oregon coast, we get a *lot* of rain! After I slog through the mud, my hip and back pain is getting unbearable."

The only sounds were eight-month-old Hazel's fingernails scraping on her highchair tray . . . and Dad's excited voice.

"Finally, we have our chance to farm!"

Silence hung in the air for only a moment. "Where?" Frank asked. "When are we moving? What do . . ."

"Slow down," Dad interrupted. "I can't answer that fast." He grinned. "We're going to the Columbia Basin Irrigation Project . . ."

That meant nothing to me. By the blank looks on Frank's and Emma's faces, it probably didn't mean much to them either. Mom's face showed no expression. Her eyes looked darker than usual. I couldn't begin to guess what she was thinking.

". . . in southeastern Washington," Dad continued. "About three hundred miles east and a little north of here. The place is pretty much a desert now, according to what I've read. But the government built Grand Coulee Dam on the Columbia River in northern Washington. Now they've dug canals so irrigation water can flow hundreds of miles to lots of farms. And they're selling farms to veterans."

"But you didn't go to war, did you?" Frank asked.

"No, I didn't. I helped the war effort by working with my folks on their farm."

"So, how's this affect us?" Frank persisted.

Dad held up his hands as if to slow the barrage. "Here's how. Your Uncle Max was in the navy. When I read about the farms, I told him. He said, 'I don't want to farm.' And I said, 'That's what I thought. But how about if you apply for a farm? If you get it, I'll farm it.'

"So he applied for eighty acres. And he got it!" Dad's eyes lit up even brighter. "So we're moving out of the rain! We're going to the sunshine!" He paused. "Remember the stories we've read about early pioneers?"

"Yeah," Emma and Frank agreed.

"Well, this will be kind of like pioneering," Dad said. He paused. His smile disappeared and his eyes narrowed. "Money will be tight at first," he said, "but we'll sell our place here." He smiled again. "Then, this fall we'll harvest our crops and have the farm income." He chuckled. "Yep," he assured us, "we'll break sod and turn our little corner of the desert into a productive farm!"

Frank's eyes sparkled like he was catching Dad's enthusiasm. Emma looked bewildered. "So, when are we moving?"

"Right after Frank graduates from eighth grade."

One of Emma's eyebrows crooked up. "That's only a couple weeks away."

"Yep." Dad grinned. "Got to get crops planted this spring so we can have a harvest this fall." He paused, then went on. "So, you're going to need to help Mom pack."

The next morning Dad brought a pile of boxes into the kitchen. "What are all the boxes for?" I asked Mom.

"So we can take our things with us when we move."

"But we don't usually take this much stuff when we go for a trip."

Mom sat down on a kitchen chair and motioned me close. "We're not just going on a trip," she said. "We're going to go live in a different place."

I looked around the kitchen. "We won't come home?"

"No, we'll live in a new place."

"Will we take our house with us?"

"No." She sighed. "I wish we could."

The next couple weeks went by in a blur. Dad parked the big 1946 army-green Chevy truck next to the shop. Previously it had been used to haul logs or logging equipment. Dad and Frank built rails on the sides of the truck's flat bed. Then they loaded it with tools and rough-sawed boards. In the house, we filled boxes with our belongings.

As the days passed, we visited friends and relatives spread around Gilbert Creek and Gopher Valley—there were more hugs than usual when we left each family. For some reason, Mom didn't smile as much as usual.

Personally, I told my troubles to Smokey. The big, woolly dog's eyes were clouded with years—years full of giving love to and being loved by every family member. Even though he was nearly deaf, telling him all about the upcoming move comforted me.

Frank graduated on a Tuesday evening. Early the next morning, Dad double-checked that the load on the truck was fastened down well. After breakfast, he and Frank crawled into the truck and drove off.

Mom and Emma kept packing boxes. A week after Dad and Frank left, they returned.

"Got the place ready for habitation," Dad said.

"What's it like?" Emma asked.

"Kinda flat and kinda dry," Dad answered. "But we'll make a farm out of it."

"And we built a house!" Frank enthused. "And there's pavement. We built the house on an old airstrip. I even found a bomb!"

Mom's eyes popped wide open. "You found what?"

Frank's eyes sparkled. "A bomb!"

"Don't worry," Dad said. "They aren't live bombs. Just practice bombs filled with water to simulate the weight and fall of a real bomb. It was for training navy pilots during World War II. No planes landing there now and no bombs falling."

Mom looked at Dad with a strange expression.

CHAPTER 2

Into the Unknown

T he next day I watched nine-month-old Hazel while everyone else loaded goods onto the big truck with the siderails
and into the pickup with its canopy. Then Dad and Frank
built a small pen in the back corner of the truck. With Hazel's toys
packed in some box somewhere, I carried her as I wandered around
the yard. I picked a dandelion and tickled her nose with it. She giggled, we sat down in the flowers, and she reached for more. We picked
daisies, looked at the waterfall, looked for ripe wild strawberries.

Early the following morning, in June of 1954, Dad, Mom,
Emma, and Frank loaded our beds onto the truck, then two milk
goats and a half dozen sheep into the pen in the back, left corner of
the truck bed. Mom pushed a few more boxes and miscellaneous
small items under the canopy of our white 1950 Ford pickup,
until almost every nook and cranny was filled. The lunch basket
went in last.

Hazel and I looked for Smokey, but he was nowhere to be found.

"Time to go!" Dad announced.

"Where's Smokey?" I asked. "We can't leave Smokey."

Dad's Adam's apple squiggled. He swallowed hard. "Smokey won't be going with us."

Something about Dad's voice and the set of his jaw told me not to ask any more questions.

Mom crawled into the driver's seat of the pickup. "Frank," Dad said, "you ride with Mom and the girls for a while. Keep an eye on the truckload to make sure everything's riding okay. With the canopy on the pickup, that load should be okay, but check once in a while to be sure." Dad turned to Mom. "If there's a problem, blink the headlights 'till I notice and I'll pull over."

We kids climbed into the pickup. Dad headed the truck up our driveway hill. When he started down the gravel road, clouds of dust billowed up. Mom and Frank rolled up their windows quickly. I wondered how the animals could breathe.

We bounced along, leaving behind the Gilbert Creek settlement—our church, school, gym, friends, grandparents, aunts, uncles, and cousins. The racks on the truck swayed with the bumps, but everything held together. "So far, so good," Frank said.

We passed a road we'd driven often to Dad's parents' farm. "When will we get to see Papa and Grandmommy again?" I asked.

"I don't know," Mom answered.

"It's especially sad leaving with Grandmommy being sick," Emma added.

"She doesn't act sick," I said.

"You're right," Mom said. "She doesn't act sick. She's never been a complainer. But she has a cancer tumor that's already spread, so she'll probably get much sicker before we get to see her again."

A sad silence filled the cab of the pickup. Shortly we passed the cemetery where Grandpa Miller and other of Mom's relatives were buried.

"Will Grandma Miller come see us this summer?" Emma asked.

"I wish she could have come before we moved," Mom said. "But a teacher has to stay and finish up after the students are done with their school year."

Frank kept an eye on the truckload ahead. When we left the gravel road with its ruts and bumps, Frank announced, "Nothing's fallen out so far." He turned and looked behind again. "Looking good in the pickup, too."

We passed the lumber mill where Dad had hauled many loads of logs, then we drove through Willamina—past its general store where I'd first seen the doll buggy that was my gift the previous Christmas. Past Sheridan the woods broke open and pastures and hayfields flanked the road, along with orchards of prunes, walnuts, and filberts. Then McMinnville—Mac to us locals. Mac was about twenty-five miles from our house—the "big city" where we shopped for major purchases.

Emma poked Frank on the leg. "There's the hospital where we were born."

A few blocks later Frank pointed to the other side of Main Street. "And there's Colvin Ford where we bought our pickup brand-spankin' new."

We passed the grocery store where we did major grocery shopping for the things we didn't grow in our garden or buy at the small store in Willamina.

Leaving town, we approached the turn to Gaston. Emma looked at Mom. "Isn't Gaston where you were born?"

"Yes," she answered. "Born there, went to school there." She glanced left up the road we'd taken many times.

"Is that where you were valedictorian of your senior class?"

"Yes." A slight smile edged the corners of Mom's mouth. It was the first I'd seen her smile all day. "Lived all my life in this country," she added.

"Isn't that where you roomed with Aunt Verda?" Frank asked.

"Yes!" Mom ginned wider. "We had oodles of fun."

"Where Dad would say he was going to see his sister, but he was really coming to see you?" Frank added.

Mom chuckled. "Yes, that was where it was."

We drove through Newberg.

"What's it like where we're going," Emma asked Frank.

Frank's eyes lit up. "It's an adventure!"

"But what's it like?"

8

"Well . . . it's kinda dry. And kinda flat." He paused, then shook his head. "I can't describe it. You'll just have to wait and see."

"Tell me," she begged. "Don't tease!"

"I'm not teasing. I don't know how to describe it." He paused. "You'll see it soon enough. Then you can describe it to yourself."

Why can't he describe it? I wondered.

Finally, we arrived in Portland—the Oregon city where Dad sometimes went to get parts for his logging equipment or for the lumber mill he and Mom had owned along with Mom's brother and sister and their spouses. If our family went along and we were in Portland over lunchtime and Mom hadn't packed a lunch, we'd stop at Ross's Health Food store for yummy sandwiches and milkshakes.

But that day we went right on through Portland. Sometimes a red light stopped us at an intersection and Dad and the truck got ahead of us. "Will we know where to go?" I wondered aloud.

"Dad won't let us get too far behind," Mom assured us.

"Besides," Frank announced, "I know where to go anyway!"

Mom was right. Dad and the truck weren't very far ahead of us as we headed east out of Portland. But it seemed like we lagged behind the truck. "Can't you drive closer to Dad?" I asked.

"Yes," Mom answered, "but with our loads, we're going slower than most of the cars. With all these curves, if cars tried to pass both of us at once they might run into a car coming the other way. It'll be easier if they can pass us one at a time. Don't you think we ought to be thoughtful of other drivers?"

"Yeah," I agreed. That was just like Mom—always caring about other people.

After a while we drove beside the Columbia River. On the far side, hills rose above the water. At first there were lots of trees beside the road. Then fewer. It looked so different than our home in the woods. I already missed the majestic forest and the beautiful trillium and fern.

"Is this what it's like where we're going?" I asked.

"No." Frank shook his head.

Finally, we stopped in The Dalles at a service station. Frank jumped out of the pickup. "Loads are riding fine!" he hollered as Dad approached.

"Wonderful!" Dad said. He turned toward us in the pickup. "We've gone about 150 miles. We're about halfway to the farm."

I sighed. It was going to be a long day.

Dad double-checked both loads. An attendant filled the gas tanks. We made good use of the restrooms and guzzled water at the drinking fountain. Frank replenished the tubs of water for the animals. The sheep and goats bleated their thanks.

"We'll stop up the road a piece for lunch," Dad said, "at Celilo Falls." Then he asked, "Frank, want to ride with me now?"

"Absolutely!" He shot a sly glance into the pickup cab. "Be glad to get away from all these girls!"

"Good riddance!" Emma responded.

At Celilo Falls, water cascaded over huge rocks and through a narrow crevasse. "Emma, would you hang onto Hazel?" Mom asked.

"She'd be a goner," Dad added, "if she crawled to the edge and fell off this cliff into the water."

"And the rest of you," Mom added. "Stay away from the edge!"

Emma carried Hazel as we walked across the solid rock, then sat down. The roar of the falls sounded so loud I could hardly hear Dad say the blessing on our food. Mom pulled a wet washcloth out of a plastic bag. We knew the routine. Frank grabbed it, washed his hands, and passed the washcloth on to Emma. "Ready for food!" he said.

As soon as we wiped any grime off our hands, Mom handed us a sandwich. While we ate, we watched fishermen make their way out over the falls on wooden walkways and reach far down into the water with nets on long poles. "Those poles must be twenty feet long," Dad said.

Some men climbed into rickety wooden baskets hanging from cables, then rode over raging water to other rock outcroppings.

Mom, Dad, or Emma held onto Hazel at all times.

It didn't take long to eat sandwiches, carrots, and the cookies Emma had made. Dad stood up. "Let's hit the road!" Mom handed us each an apple to eat on the way and closed up the lunch basket.

The day wore on. As we drove, Mom told stories. Sometimes we girls chatted. Emma held Hazel most of the time. Emma was a quiet, steady, dependable young woman. Ordinarily, the biggest to-do she made about anything was simply defending herself from our pesky brother.

Sometimes I held Hazel for a while. We played patty-cake till I hoped I'd never hear patty-cake again. When she got restless and started to reach for the steering wheel, I handed her back to Emma.

Before long we left behind all trees except for an occasional skinny, dry-looking bush. "They're juniper trees," Mom said.

To me, they looked like a poor excuse for a tree.

The day got hotter with each mile. The sheep and goats panted as they lay in their pen on the truck ahead of us. The sun seemed to bake us. Even the wind blowing in the open windows felt hot. And it smelled different—no sweet forest fragrance like at home. I drew in a deep breath, trying to identify the odor—it smelled like . . . dust.

The farther we drove, the more barren the land looked. Could it get any worse? What would Uncle Max's place be like?

CHAPTER 3

Little House

The highlight of the long drive came in the middle of the sizzling afternoon. Dad stopped by the side of the road in Umatilla, Oregon. Mom pulled the pickup in behind him. "Anyone hot?" Dad hollered.

"Yes!" we chorused.

We piled out. Dad went into the roadside stand, then came out with orange popsicles. He handed us each a cold treat on a stick. Shortly the sweat ran down our faces and the hot air melted drops off the popsicles. We licked the sides to keep them from melting all over us. I savored the sweet coolness.

Back on the road, we jostled on along the Columbia River, passed the "Entering Washington" sign, and turned northwest at Wallula Junction. Every mile felt like forever.

We bounced on to Pasco, then straight north on a gravel road. Desert seemed to stretch to the ends of the earth. "Dad said the farm is only twenty miles from Pasco." Mom sighed. "Shouldn't be much farther."

Matthew's Corner was the first sign of civilization since we'd left Pasco. Two lights on a tall pole stood over a building and a scale for weighing trucks. A quarter mile further, we turned left, crossed a water canal, bore to the right, and drove a couple hundred feet on two tracks of sand. Scattered tufts of skinny grass and small gray-green bushes I'd never before seen dotted the sand.

Dad stopped the truck on a wide patch of black pavement. Mom pulled the pickup beside the truck. I looked around . . . dumbfounded.

Frank hopped out of the truck and bounced toward the passenger side of the pickup, wearing a grin. Dad strolled to the driver's side and announced, "We're home!"

I gawked at the strange surroundings. It didn't look like home to me!

Hazel slept on the seat behind me.

Emma gazed left and right, front and back, brows furrowing deeper by the second.

Mom stared out the window. Silent. Lifeless.

Finally, Emma exploded the silence with a puzzled, "Where's the house?"

"There!" Frank announced with pride and smug wisdom. He pointed to a small shack.

The tiny structure looked like the sheepherder's shack we had seen when we'd visited friends in eastern Oregon the previous year—a tiny shack on wheels that a sheepherder could tow behind a truck or pickup when they moved their flock of sheep to a new pasture. Only this shack didn't have wheels.

I stared. It wasn't even big enough to hold our beds. I looked around. The place didn't look anything like home. To me, home was our white house with red geraniums in window boxes. Home was surrounded by trees and mountains.

Mom, Emma, and I tumbled out of the pickup, too full of questions to know where to begin. A warm breeze hit my face. Dad led us toward the shack.

"We built it with lap boards," Frank declared as we walked. He pointed to the vertical boards on the side of the shack. "We put one-by-fours over the cracks between boards to be sure and keep out rain . . . and the bugs."

One of Emma's eyebrows jutted up. "Do they *ever* get rain here?" she sneered.

Dad cleared his throat—the throat clearing that meant we're not going any further with that topic. He swung the door open toward the inside.

"It's eight feet wide and sixteen feet long," Dad explained as he motioned Mom and the rest of us inside. "Plenty of room for a kitchen."

The door was on the south end, the end closest to the truck and pickup. Plain boards made a wood counter along the wall on the right. One shelf was under the counter. Two small windows let in light—one on the east side above the counter and one on the north end, opposite the door. Open shelves hung against the wall on either side of the window over the counter and the window on the north wall.

"There's not room enough for our beds," I blurted.

"You're right," Dad answered, "but I've got a plan. By bedtime, you'll have a bed."

I looked around, baffled.

"Anyone need the bathroom?" Dad asked.

The "bathroom" was no place for a bath—it was an outhouse a jaunt north off the edge of the pavement. A gallon can nailed to the wall held a roll of toilet paper. The outhouse had no roof. "No one's looking down from up there," Dad said.

It didn't take long to tour the whole facility—the kitchen shack, an outhouse, and a pen for the sheep and goats. That was it, except for the view—to the south, a slight barren rise held a westbound irrigation canal. To the east, north, and west, sagebrush and cheatgrass seemed to stretch to the end of the world. Occasional tumbleweeds danced across the desert in the breeze. Not a tree in sight in any direction. The closest things to trees were the poles for the electric power line paralleling the road and, fortunately, a pole by our kitchen shack.

"I need to wet my whistle," Dad said. He poured a glass of water out of a ten-gallon milk can sitting just outside the shack door. "Anyone else want a drink of water?" he asked, holding a glass toward us.

I was hot and tired. Probably everybody else was too. We took him up on the offer.

"It's lukewarm. May not taste the greatest," Dad said. "But let me warn you now—don't drink the irrigation water! Besides having fish swimming in it, there's other stuff that can make you sick." He paused. "But there's a well house about a mile from here with clean drinking water where we can go anytime. Only drink water out of these cans."

He was right about lukewarm water not tasting great. But at least it was wet.

Most of the truckload of goods would have to wait till the next day, but some things were essential for the night—like beds. We unloaded animals first and enclosed them in the pen Dad and Frank had prepared. Frank grabbed a bucket and headed to the ditch we'd crossed. He carried water to the animals and poured it into a tub. They crowded around, noses down, and made sounds like several people sucking ravenously through large straws. He carried several buckets of water to the animals before they were satisfied and there was enough in the tubs to meet their thirst overnight.

Next off the truck came a heavy pile of canvas. While I watched Hazel, everyone else unfolded the gray-green canvas. Then Dad gave directions. Working together, slowly a large army-surplus tent took shape southwest of the shack.

After raising the tent, while Dad and the older kids hauled bedsteads, mattresses, and the baby's crib to the tent, I "helped" Mom get out what was left of the pile of sandwiches she'd made that morning before we'd left home. Mom hollered for the others, Dad said the blessing, and we each grabbed a sandwich. They were a little dry, but nobody complained—we were, after all, hot, tired, and famished.

After supper we set up beds in the tent. We got bedding from the truck. The summer sun set while we made the beds.

It had been a long day. And we'd come a long way—in a direction I wasn't much impressed with so far. But here I was. And I'd have time to think about the contrasts another day. Besides, it was too dark to even think.

I was nearly asleep when shrill screams startled me. I lay in bed, scared to move. Suddenly I valued sharing a bed with my older sister. But she seemed to be holding her breath. Was she afraid too?

Another wail shattered the night. Then silence. Then several more screams. Shivers raced down my spine. I held my breath. Scared to make a sound, but too scared not to, I finally hollered, "What's that?"

"Nothing to worry about," Dad called from the other end of the tent. "Just coyotes. They're off a ways. They'll sing you to sleep."

I didn't like their music. I wasn't cold, but I pulled the covers tighter around my shoulders and lay there listening . . . until the haunting coyote chorus crept into dreams. Or was it the beginning of a nightmare?

CHAPTER 4

New Normal

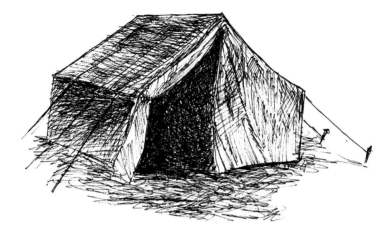

I stretched as I woke. After a yawn and another stretch, I lay still . . . listening. What were the strange sounds?

Mom's hushed voice. And Dad's voice. Birds—different bird sounds than I was used to hearing through the window open to our woods. What was going on? I opened my eyes. It was dark. Not black dark, but too dark to see clearly. I felt rested—like it should be morning—but why was it so dark? I looked around. As my eyes adjusted to the darkness, I saw the shadowy figure of my sister getting dressed.

In an instant, yesterday poured itself into my mind: Leaving home. The long, hot trip. The shack Frank called a house. The big, army-green tent going up over hot pavement. The coyotes howling.

Just then, Frank opened a tent flap and looked out. "Morning, world!" Light flooded in and the sad memories of the day before looked all too real.

Dad pulled the other door flap aside and stuck his head in. "Up and at 'em!" he hollered.

I crawled out of bed and donned the same clothes I'd worn yesterday—our other clothes were on the truck . . . somewhere.

"Don't forget to make your bed," Mom reminded.

Hm-m-m. Living in a tent isn't going to change the rules any.

Frank headed out to milk the goats and feed and water them and the sheep. Emma dressed Hazel, and Mom went to the shack to fix a simple breakfast.

At breakfast Frank complained, "I thought those coyotes would never stop howling last night! They woke me up several times."

"Me too," Emma said. "They sounded like they were just on the other side of the canvas!"

"Right after we went to bed?" I asked.

"Not just then," Frank blurted. "They howled half the night."

"Or more," Emma added.

"I only heard them when we first went to bed," I said.

"That's about right," Mom concluded. "Once you go to sleep, you sleep about as sound as a rock."

"Yeah," Emma added. "A building could collapse around you, and you'd still be snoring."

When we'd finished breakfast, Mom said, "Helen, will you please play with Hazel? Keep her out of the way while we unload the truck, so she doesn't get hurt." She handed Hazel to me and started to turn away. Then she wheeled back and raised her voice. "And don't go anywhere near the canal!" she commanded. "She could drown!"

I carried Hazel off a ways, where we could be safe but still watch the goings on. Dad backed the truck near the door at the end of the shack. "I hope they don't drop that!" I said as Dad, Mom, Emma, and Frank slid the refrigerator down off the truck and "walked" it in the door. "Whew! They made it," I chattered to my charge. "Here comes the kitchen stove." Our family movers repeated the process with the electric range.

"Here comes the table," I told Hazel as Dad and Emma handed it down to Mom and Frank. Chairs followed. "Look!" I told Hazel. "There's your highchair. I guess you get to eat, too."

Hazel clapped her hands, giggled, or chattered unintelligibly in response to my commentary and the unusual activity.

Next, boxes of various sizes and shapes were unloaded into the shack.

Bored, Hazel started to crawl away. I wished Smokey was there to help entertain her. I picked her up and we wandered aimlessly over the black pavement, then onto sand. Ouch! Those tumbleweeds were stickery! I stepped carefully to avoid them. There wasn't much to see . . . until I looked closer. "Look!" I exclaimed. I leaned over and pointed to the horned toad zipping across the sand. Hazel spotted the movement, waved her arms, and giggled.

Eventually, Dad moved the truck away from the shack and toward the tent door. The movers unloaded chests of drawers into the tent. And more boxes. Hazel and I wandered around till the sun shone hot from straight above. Our stomachs growled quite a while before Mom finally called, "Dinner's ready."

That afternoon, the rest of the boxes and equipment were unloaded off the truck. Hazel took an afternoon nap in her crib in the tent. I quietly tidied things in my drawers and listened for Hazel to wake. Dad and Frank loaded the five-gallon and ten-gallon milk cans into the pickup and drove off to fill them with clean drinking water.

"Cool water," Dad called when they got back. Everyone came and enjoyed the cool, refreshing water. It only took the first drink the previous day to learn that after the cans stood for a few hours in the sun, their contents were nauseatingly warm.

Few clouds shaded us from the sun. To make it even hotter, the black pavement absorbed the sun's heat and reflected it upward. Sometimes a breeze helped to ease the heat a little, but often even the breeze felt hot.

By the end of the afternoon, we were all hot and sweaty. "Why don't you get your swimming suits on and go cool off in the canal?" Mom suggested to us three older kids. "Stay together and watch out for each other."

We were happy to comply!

"And take your washcloth and this soap along," Mom urged. "Have a bath while you're there." She paused. "Supper will be ready when you get back."

Within a couple days Mom had organized the kitchen and Dad had strung rope in a couple spots across the tent. Mom found the boxes of curtains and extra blankets. She and Emma hung them on the ropes while I handed them large safety pins to hold the curtains in place. Mom and Dad shared their "room" on the west end of the tent with Hazel and her crib. Emma and I shared the double bed and room on the east end and Frank's room was in the middle. I found my two dolls and set them on top of our chest of drawers. Emma added a couple perfume bottles to the other end. On his chest of drawers, Frank proudly displayed the balsa wood model airplane he'd painstakingly built and carefully packed.

It felt good to get our belongings unpacked—at least as many as we could find places for.

Frank felt sorry for his panting sheep in their wooly coats. He found his hand clippers and headed to the sheep pen.

Frank had started his flock one summer back in Oregon when he'd helped Papa—our grandpa—with some farm projects. At the end of the job, Papa said, "You can have either a twenty-dollar bill or a ewe." Frank chose the sheep. When his ewe produced a little buck, he sold it; when she had a ewe lamb, he kept it. Thus, his little flock grew.

The first time Frank sheared a sheep's winter coat several years earlier, it took him half a day—both he and the sheep were worn out at the end of the process. Besides, the poor sheep had a few nicks in her skin, and she surely was embarrassed by her rough looking clip. Both Frank's skills and speed improved with practice. By this summer, he held a sheep on its rear between his knees. He pulled the wool away with his left hand and snip, snip, snipped with the hand clippers in his right hand. Each sheep jumped up and bounced off when he freed them, seeming pleased to be free of the jacket they didn't need in the hot desert sun.

The sheep weren't the only hot creatures. After the sun had shone down on it all day, inside the tent the temperature sizzled! No one wanted many blankets when we first went to bed. But we were tired enough that the bed felt good anyway.

The closest neighbor was the scale house for weighing trucks, about a half a mile away at Matthew's Corner. The site also included a tiny store and a phone booth. At night we could see the two lights on tall poles.

The only other close neighbor was nearly a mile north of our place. We couldn't see any buildings, but we could see the wind whip up dust behind his tractor when he worked his field.

That weekend on the way to church, we saw that a new bridge over the Columbia River between Pasco and Kennewick was under construction.

After church, a couple invited our whole family to their house for dinner. The husband and wife were both schoolteachers—the father would probably be Frank's and Emma's schoolteacher come fall. Their son, Dale, was Frank's age and in the same school grade. At first, they were both quiet, but before the afternoon was over, Frank and Dale chattered away like long-lost friends. As we drove away late in the afternoon, Dale and Frank hollered at each other, "See you next week!" On the way home, Frank couldn't stop talking about his new friend.

Within a few days, Dad also built a clothesline just north and west of the shack, off the pavement. With temperatures soaring, people sweating, and cotton diapers to wash, the clothesline came none too soon.

CHAPTER 5

Again

With a clothesline built, it was time to wash clothes. Laundry was an all-day project. Mom heated water in the big canning kettle on the electric kitchen range, then lugged it outside to the wringer washer. She added soap and a load of laundry, plugged the washer into an electric cord, and the paddles swished back and forth, back and forth. While it worked, she heated another canner of water to fill the rinse tub.

After the agitator had swished the laundry for a while, she ran the clothing, one piece at a time, through the wringer. Each piece dropped into the tub of rinse water. She rinsed them by hand, then ran them through the wringer again. She and Emma carried them in a second tub to the clothesline and hung each piece. I couldn't reach the lines, but I handed clothespins to whoever hung the various pieces.

Load followed load—dishtowels first, then whites, then light colors, then dark colors. By the end of the day, the white dishtowels, the white diapers, and clothes of every hue and size fluttered in the breeze. With the sun shining hot and the breeze blowing warm, the dishtowels and diapers dried within an hour or two, dresses took longer. Heavy overalls took even longer to dry—we usually left them on the clothesline overnight and they'd be dry in the morning.

Planting a garden was also high on Mom's priority list. She'd always grown a big garden. The dark, rich, loamy soil of our hillside garden back home grew large amounts of produce—peas, carrots, beets, turnips, spinach, green beans, lettuce, radishes, cabbage, corn, and other vegetables. We kids had weeded. We helped pick. We shelled peas and snapped beans. We cleaned vegetables and made salads. Our family had all the vegetables we could eat fresh. Mom shared some, stored what she could for later, and canned hundreds of quarts of vegetables for winter use.

Mom had brought along seed so she could plant the garden quickly. Frank and Emma spaded a small garden area by hand. Well, they tried to. But the sand had no body—the whole shovelful just ran back into the hole. Emma pulled a hoe at an angle. Mom followed her, dropping seeds just behind the hoe. As they moved forward, the sand drifted over the seeds, and no one would ever know where the rows were except for the stakes Mom put at each end.

Dad attached a sprinkler to a garden hose, and the hose to a small pump which he placed at the ditch. He started the pump, and the sprinkler in the garden dampened a circle of sand to a darker tan.

Sure enough, like Dad had said, the sun and water did wonders to the desert. Within a few days, seedlings began peeking out of the warm sand.

"I'm glad the garden's growing," he told Mom, "But we have to get a tractor if we're going to have a crop." He listened to a radio program where people offered items for sale or to give away. When he got a newspaper, he scoured the ads for equipment. He made the rounds of farm equipment dealers. Then he heard about a family who wanted to sell a tractor and went to look for it one afternoon.

At supper after his jaunt, he reported. "I had trouble finding the people who wanted to sell the tractor, so I drove into one place where I saw some equipment. Couldn't believe my eyes! There were several little kids, and they were running in and out of a huge pile of tumbleweeds. Their arms and legs were bare. *How can they do that?* I thought. *They must be getting scratched up something fierce!* My skin hurt for them." He shook his head. "Why? Why would they be running in and out of a pile of tumbleweeds?"

He let the picture gel in our minds, then went on. "Then a woman walked out of the tumbleweed mountain."

Both Emma and Frank frowned.

"Yep," Dad said. He grinned. "The family is living in a tent. Theirs is probably as hot as ours. So they gathered tumbleweeds and piled them up over their tent to try to block some of the sun!"

"Will it work?" Frank asked.

"I don't know," Dad said, "but as folks are moving in, they're doing whatever they have to to make a go of farming."

Days came and went. They began to blur one into another. Life settled into a routine. In the morning, Dad read aloud to the family from a devotional book, he prayed for our day and asked a blessing on our food, then we dove into breakfast. Dinner was at noon, listening to *Paul Harvey News and Commentary* on the radio. Supper about 6:00 p.m. Between meals different ones worked at different projects. Before bed, we gathered around the table and Dad led a short Bible study. We worked on memorizing a Bible verse. Dad prayed, then Mom, Emma, Frank, and, finally, me.

Twice a day, someone—usually Emma or Frank—milked the goats and fed and watered all the animals. Mom strained the milk, then put it in jars in the refrigerator.

Goat milk was an important commodity at our house. Months before when Hazel was tiny, she wasn't growing well. It was a serious enough problem that Mom and Dad took her to the doctor—an unusual occurrence for any of us. After examining her and asking questions, the doctor said, "Seems she may have a problem with cow's milk. Doesn't someone up in those hills have some goats?"

"Yeah," Dad said, "*we* have goats out in the woods to help keep the brush down."

"Catch one," the doctor exclaimed, "and give this poor child something she can digest!"

Dad caught a couple goats, kept them away from their kids, and started milking them. Sure enough. Baby Hazel began growing and, by the time of our move to the desert, was a healthy, active, bright-eyed nine-month-old. We brought the goats along, and they each had a kid. Frank's sheep had lambs too. That year Dad kept a billy goat kid and Frank kept a buck lamb. The animal pen was full of bleats, ba-a-as, and romping.

At first after our move, the sheep and goats got along fine in one pen. They ate from the same food trough and drank from the same water tub. But one morning at breakfast, Frank cocked his head, then asked, "What's that?"

Emma looked sidelong at Frank. "What's what?"

"That thudding sound."

Everyone stopped chewing and listened.

Thud . . . silence . . . thud . . . silence . . . thud . . .

Dad grinned. "Bet you'll figure out what it is if you go look at the animals."

Frank got up from the table and walked out the door. Silence. He returned, sat down, and took a bite of oatmeal. "Don't know what it is."

"You'll see soon enough," Dad responded.

We continued our breakfast.

"There it is again," Frank blurted through his mouthful of oatmeal mush. He scooted his chair back and jumped up in one movement. Out the door he went.

Sure enough, there was that sound again. Thud . . . silence . . . thud . . . silence . . . thud . . . silence . . . thud . . .

Frank was outside only a moment before he came back to the table. "The ram and billy goat are dueling," he said.

After breakfast, I went to see the antics that made the noise. The young ram and young billy goat eyed each other. The ram backed up, lowered his head, and ran toward the goat. The billy goat reared up on his hind legs, and the two slammed into each other's skulls. Thud. Then they backed up, eyed each other again, and proceeded. Thud . . . silence . . . thud . . . silence . . . thud . . . silence . . . thud . . . became monotonous.

Every day or two, Dad went after drinking water. Mom cooked three hearty meals a day, washed mounds of laundry, ground grain, baked bread, kept tabs on the garden, and tried to keep peace between four hot siblings from nine months old to sixteen years. I helped with many of the projects. Often, my job was to keep tabs on the youngest, keeping her away from the irrigation canals full of water. Emma and Frank were usually in the middle of some of the work.

Six days a week there was weeding to do in the garden. And there was always cooking. Heating water, then washing dishes in one dishpan, rinsing them in another, and drying them. We carried the dishwater to the garden and emptied it onto the ground by plants, then rinsed the dishpan with the rinse water and watered more plants. Every drop of water was precious.

I wished we had more of it—like for a bathtub and a flush toilet. In our house in the woods, we'd had indoor plumbing, but some friends of our family did not. As a little girl, I was fascinated by their outhouse. Whenever our family visited them, I always *needed* to use it. Now that an outhouse was our only toileting facility, the fascination wore off quickly!

Spiders appreciated the outhouse more than I did. They fashioned fancy webs worthy of admiration. If only they would have spun them someplace else—fighting through their newest cobweb creations was bad enough. Their abundant supply of flies and other insects caught in the webs was disgusting.

Weeks came and went. We listened to *Paul Harvey News and Commentary* and to local news. We worked, attended church, went to church picnics—they always boasted plenty of good food and generally included a softball game. Dad and Frank both loved to play softball and would be in the thick of it. Dale enjoyed playing ball, too. Whether it came to softball or food, Dale and Frank spent more and more time together.

Whenever we were near the new bridge construction, we gawked and surmised about when it would open for traffic. A surplus store in Kennewick, where Dad purchased things occasionally, would be easier to drive to once the new bridge was completed.

On the way home from one picnic, Frank announced, "I'm looking forward to school. I'm glad Dale's dad will be my teacher. He really seems to like us kids."

"School?" Emma rolled her eyes. "You can have it."

At home late one afternoon Mom and Emma finished hanging wet laundry on the line, then hurried to get supper. Hungry, the family gathered. The usual breeze strengthened. Soon the wind blew hard. The clothes on the line flew horizontally. "The clothes should dry fast today," Emma remarked.

Just before supper was ready, Frank looked out the open door. "What's that?" he bellowed.

Dad walked to the door. "Oh-oh!" He groaned. "It's one of the dust storms I've heard about."

Mom stepped to the door. Her face contorted. "Get the laundry!" she ordered.

Emma and I jumped up from the table. All of us raced toward the clothesline. The sky to the west boiled brown.

Suddenly, the gale hit full force. Desert sand blasted us. In an instant, our eyes felt gritty. The wind howled. The air became an eerie, yellow-brown, churning mass. We couldn't see the row of light poles by the road.

"Get inside," Mom hollered. "It's too late for the laundry."

We reversed direction and ran toward the shack. The last one in slammed the door, but the air inside already smelled like dirt. A layer of dust covered the counter, the table, and our dishes. Mom's shoulders drooped.

Several of us gazed out the two windows. The air churned yellow. Tumbleweeds bounced across the landscape at a dizzying pace. Mom rinsed off our plates, dried them, and set them back on the table. "Let's eat," she said. We sat around the table in our regular places. There wasn't a lot of conversation, but it wasn't quiet. The wind shrieked and screamed. The sand blasted against the wall.

We stayed in the shack while the wind howled outside. Dad read aloud to us—reading was a frequent family pastime, the shack provided protection from the storm, and it was good to have something else to think about.

The wind died down eventually. Just before we headed off to bed in the tent, Mom sighed. "I hope the garden survives."

While still in bed the next morning, I heard Mom say, "Some of the plants look pretty bedraggled. Could you get the sprinkler going on the garden first thing?"

"I will," Dad said. "Right away."

The dishtowels and diapers on the clothesline, so bright white the afternoon before, were the tan color of desert sand. My red dress looked tan with a red tinge. All the clothes were tan . . . and gritty.

At breakfast Mom looked at Dad. "We're going to need more water this morning." She sighed. "We have to do every bit of the laundry all over again."

CHAPTER 6

Let the Farming Begin

"That plow sitting out there won't do us a smidgen of good until we get a tractor," Dad announced one evening at supper. "And I think I may have found one we can afford. I'll go check it out in the morning."

He and Frank took off in the truck after breakfast. Just before dinnertime at noon they returned. Dad backed the truck up tight against a ditch-bank road and backed a grey tractor off the truck. He drove the truck to the shack and Frank, smiling from ear to ear, followed him on the tractor. They hitched up the plow.

"The tractor's a Ford 8N," Dad said as we started eating. "It's pretty small, but it should do the job for now."

After dinner Dad and Frank headed west from the shack. A while later, Dad came walking back, but the drone of the tractor continued.

Mom looked concerned. "Are you sure Frank's okay?"

"He'll do fine," Dad answered. "Remember, he's been driving the D6 Caterpillar up the hillsides in Oregon. This tractor's a lot smaller . . . and he's on flat land." Dad snickered. "Not a hillside for him to fall off for miles around."

Mom grinned. "You can say that again!"

As suppertime approached, Mom had me do one of my usual jobs—set the table. Hurrying to get out of the hot shack where Mom had been cooking, I dropped silverware haphazardly near their usual places.

Mom turned. "I don't believe that's the way you know to set the table."

"But what does it matter?"

"We are civilized people." She smiled and laid a hand on my shoulder. "We might not have the best circumstances right now," she said, "but we can make the best of the circumstances we have."

Breakfast, dinner, or supper, the criteria for the job were always the same. Our kitchen might be a strange little shack . . . sitting on a World War II airstrip . . . in the middle of a desert . . . in the center of nowhere, but Mom would settle for no disarray on the red and white checkered tablecloth. No dishes or utensils would be tossed willy-nilly on our table. Knives were to lie neatly to the right of the plate, at right angles with the edge of the table. Spoons were placed next to the knives. Forks just as tidy on the left side of the plate. Glasses stood at the point of each knife. I tidied the table till it was fit for a king . . . or a civilized family.

When Frank came in for supper, he brought a couple more "bombs" he'd unearthed. At the table, he chattered about his afternoon. "It'll take forever with this little one-bottom plow," he said, "but I got a good start!" He took another bite of Mom's homemade bread and jam. "It was so-o-o fun watching the hawks!" he enthused. "I hadn't been out there very long before a hawk started following me. It floated along behind me in the air." Frank started to raise both arms, then turned a bit so he wouldn't decapitate Emma as he outstretched his arms and demonstrated floating on air. "Then, all of a sudden . . ." Frank clapped his arms down by his sides. ". . . the hawk would fold its wings against its body and drop like a bomb."

"Did it touch the ground?" Dad asked.

"No. Just before it hit the ground, it spread its wings, its feet came down, it grabbed a small animal like a mouse or something and flew off with it in its talons. I wouldn't even see the mouse before the hawk caught it."

"Well," Dad said, "you did have a few other things to watch— like going straight beside where you'd just plowed."

"Yeah."

"And," Dad added, "there's another part of the story too. I was just reading the other day that birds of prey can probably see four or five times better than humans. Those hawks could probably see a mouse from the top of a ten-story building."

"Or when the hawk's just floating on air?"

"Yep. The slightest movement and a mouse doesn't have a chance."

"One less mouse to eat our crops when we get them planted," Emma added.

"Yep. Birds of prey are farmers' friends."

There was a disadvantage to plowing the desert. When the wind blew, even more dust filled the air. It settled on every surface—on our beds in the tent, on the table and chairs inside the shack, on the water in the wash pan. "When we get water on the field, it will cut down on the dust," Dad said.

Emma rolled her eyes. "I hope so!"

The next morning, Frank went back to plowing. Emma pulled uprooted sagebrush off the plowed area.

After a few days, a small field was plowed and cleared.

"I'll plant tomorrow," Dad said at supper.

"Won't you have to smooth the soil first?" Mom asked.

Dad laughed. "If we had decent soil," he said, "yes, we'd need to. But this sand flows back down till it's almost smooth." He turned toward Frank. "There are a few spots that are a little rough. In the morning, would you take the garden rake and smooth those spots?"

The next morning, Frank raked. Then Dad took a bag of oat seed and walked back and forth through the field, carefully scattering handful after handful of seed across the now-loosened ground, spreading the seed as evenly as possible. Then he took the sprinkler from the garden and started watering the oats. Every couple of hours he moved it from one spot to the next.

"We need to water the garden again," Mom urged.

"I'm almost done with the field," Dad said. "Can it wait a few more hours?"

"Yes."

The sprinkler moved across the ground until all the small field had been watered and then the garden, then it started over again in the field. In due time, the oat seeds sprouted, and a blanket of green covered the tan sand.

Finally, when I woke one morning, I heard rain on the tent. "It's raining!" I threw my corner of the covers back, jumped out of bed, and ran outside in my nightgown. I tipped my head back and let the rain run off my face. It felt cool and wonderfully refreshing. It felt like home—home in the woods. I took a deep breath. The fragrance of evergreen trees was missing, but at least the air smelled clean and fresh.

"Wayne," I heard Mom say from across the pavement, "I think you forgot one thing when you built the outhouse."

"What's that?" Dad asked.

"No one may be looking down into the outhouse from up in the sky," Mom continued, "but rain comes from that direction . . . and the toilet paper is wet."

"Hmm," Dad responded. "Sounds like I need to add a roof."

And he did. A piece of corrugated metal. So, even when we sat down in the outhouse in the middle of the day, we had shade. And on those rare occasions when rain fell, I heard music, beautiful

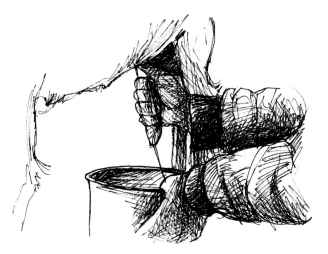

music—the same kind of music I used to hear when rain fell on the metal roof of our house in the woods.

At supper a few weeks into our desert "adventure," Dad announced, "Mom and I need to go finish up some business back home. We've got to get our Oregon property on the market!" He looked directly at my brother. "Frank, if we took the girls with us, could you hold down the fort here for a few days by yourself?"

A smile lit up Frank's face. His eyes danced. "Sure!"

"You'll need to keep the animals fed and watered and milk the goats. You'll need to keep the field and garden watered."

"I can do that. I do it every day."

"If I didn't think you could do it," Dad said, "I wouldn't consider it."

Frank smiled. It was as close to a compliment as he'd ever heard from Dad.

"Unfortunately," Mom added, "we'll be gone over your birthday."

"It's okay. I can do it," Frank assured, straightening to his full sitting height.

On Thursday, Dad, Mom, and we girls sang "Happy Birthday" to Frank a day early, then we drove off, leaving almost-fourteen-year-old Frank in charge of the farm.

The trip still felt long. But as we approached "home," the green forest had never looked so beautiful to me. The woodland air had never smelled so sweet. The wildflower colors had never looked so bright.

On Friday, Dad and Mom began dealing with the items they'd come to accomplish. Over the weekend we went to church and visited friends. On Monday and Tuesday, Dad and Mom completed their business. Wednesday—all too soon—we headed back to the desert.

Mr. Independent from the week before greeted us warmly. Then Grandma Miller walked out of the shack.

Mom's mouth dropped open when she saw her mother.

"Grandma!" we girls shouted.

"I was sure glad to see Grandma!" Frank enthused. "She knows how to cook. And she did the dishes, too!"

Mom's eyes were still big. "What are you doing here?" she asked her mother. "How did you get here?"

"It wasn't easy!"

"How did you find the place?"

"If I'd had an address, it would have helped!" Grandma's brow furrowed. "I came into Pasco on a Greyhound bus and took a taxi. From the description I remembered from your letters, the driver didn't know where you lived. We drove round and round and all over. I got a real tour of this godforsaken desert. We finally came upon your place."

"The taxi must have cost a mint!"

"The driver was kind. He turned off his meter at one point. Didn't charge me nearly as much as he could have."

"Well, welcome! Glad you found the place." Mom turned to Frank. "And how did your weekend go?

"Was glad to see Grandma! She could cook!" Frank grinned. "Besides," he added. "I didn't have all the ingredients I needed."

"Like what?"

Frank's right eyebrow jutted up. "Butter."

"Butter?"

"Yeah. Butter to put in the pan to fry pancakes in. 'Bout the only thing I know how to cook is pancakes. At first, the pancakes were fine." He shook his head. "But when I ran out of butter, they stuck in the pan. So . . . I looked around to see what I could do." He raised his hand in victory. "I spotted the paraffin candles. I melted a little wax in the frying pan and fried my pancakes."

Dad laughed. "How'd that work?"

"Worked okay." Frank's eyebrows raised and only one corner of his mouth smiled. "But I had to eat them while they were still hot or they got hard."

Mom laughed. "Well, at least you're creative!"

Grandma grimaced. "Creativity could come in handy for anyone who wants to survive in this country!"

CHAPTER 7

Wind

After the greetings, Dad wandered off to the west. He wore a
big grin when he came back. "The oats are looking good."
"And the garden looks good too," Mom added. "If we
want to eat this winter, we've got to take care of our garden." She
smiled at Frank. "Thank you for watering it well. Looks like you
even did some weeding."

Frank grinned. "Yeah, I did." His shoulders raised and his chest
puffed out.

"Careful!" Dad warned with a twinkle in his eye. "Don't pop
your buttons off!"

"That'd be hard to do with a T-shirt!" Frank responded.

Over supper Frank told us more about his weekend. His birthday treat on Friday was his specialty—paraffin-fried pancakes. By
Saturday, he was getting lonely, and he was used to going to church.
Besides, he wanted to see Dale and the other guys. After milking
the goats, he donned his suit and tie. He walked out to the road and
stuck out his thumb. So . . . there stood a barely-fourteen-year-old
boy . . . in suit and tie . . . on a Saturday morning . . . by a gravel

road . . . in the middle of the desert . . . twenty miles from town.

A car with two women stopped. The passenger rolled down her window. "Where are you going?"

"To Pasco," Frank answered. "To church."

"Climb on in."

The women were on their way to town to do some shopping. They drove out of their way to deliver Frank to the church door.

When Dale's parents found out Frank was alone for the weekend, they invited him home to dinner—a delicious meal! And he didn't have to cook it! Or do the dishes!

Frank spent a delightful afternoon with the family. Then they drove him home to the farm.

"And did I mention . . .?" Frank grinned. "Dale's mom is an excellent cook! Boy did it feel good to have a real meal." He grinned. "Besides, *no* paraffin!"

That afternoon with friends had cured Frank's problem with loneliness. He looked forward to school starting—he'd get to have more time with his new friend, Dale. And Dale's dad would be his teacher.

When Grandma Miller had arrived Monday afternoon, Frank was surprised and ecstatic. Then we arrived back at the shack on Wednesday.

That night I had a new bed partner. Grandma Miller slept with me, and Emma took a blanket to the seat of the truck. The next morning, Grandma Miller said, "The coyotes are sure noisy!"

"Did they howl last night?" I asked.

"Didn't you hear them, child?" Grandma asked with shock in her voice.

"No."

"Why, they were near loud enough to wake the dead!" Grandma retorted. How could you *not* have heard them?"

Frank spoke up. "It's the usual. Helen sleeps like she died."

"Well, I'll be," Grandma muttered as she shook her head.

Other than the new sleeping arrangements, life fell back into the same routine as before.

Looking at the animal pen one afternoon, Grandma asked, "Don't those animals ever stop butting their heads?" She shook her head. "You'd think they'd get headaches and go lie down."

"But they don't," Emma said. "They go on and on and on."

Grandma shook her head, then grinned. "They must be as hard-headed as some students I've had."

She was also amazed at other qualities of the area. "I've heard of crop rotation," she said one evening at supper, "but I've never heard of soil rotation."

"What d'ya mean?" Dad asked.

"The wind blows so much sand that by the end of the day, you have your neighbor's soil and the neighbor on the other side has yours!"

Mom laughed. "That's about right!"

Dad smirked. Finally, he said, "But at least the breeze cools the air."

"Breeze?" Grandma retorted. "Air movement at this rate is called wind!" She shook her head. "Besides," she added, "if this is cool, I'd sure hate to see what it would be like without the gale!"

Sometimes Grandma helped Mom and Emma in the kitchen. Other times she told stories to Hazel and me. Sometimes she made our desert home even less desirable than it already seemed. Trips to the outhouse, for one, got worse after one of her stories.

"Always look before you sit down!" she said. "Once when I was a girl in Montana, I went to the outhouse and discovered a big rattlesnake coiled around the opening. I nearly sat on him."

Suddenly, moonlight became insufficient for night runs to the outhouse. Keeping a flashlight by my bedside lasted beyond Grandma's two-week stay and her send-off on a Greyhound bus.

A few days later, Dad made it worse. "Watch out for the black widow spiders," he warned. "I've been hearing a lot about them lately. They're poisonous." He described them. "In fact," he added, "let's go see if we can find one so you'll know what to avoid."

We kids traipsed behind him to the outhouse. Dad went in. "Yep," he said after only a minute. "Here's a black widow. Come take a look."

He'd described it well—its shiny black body and the tiny red hourglass on its tummy. From then on, a trip to the outhouse involved a hunt for both rattlesnakes and black widow spiders. Whenever I saw a black widow, a chill went up my spine.

Our cooling-off and bathing trips to the canal nearly every afternoon were refreshing. But, when there was a break from work, the water provided another occasional pastime for Frank—fishing. One afternoon when Hazel was napping, I followed him. All was fine as long as he had his hook in the water. But then he got a bite. He pulled a fish out of the water, removed the hook from its mouth, and laid it on the ground. He turned and went back to fishing. I, on the other hand, focused on the fish. I'd never seen anything die. It flopped and writhed on the sand.

"Put the poor fish back in the water," I pled.

Frank looked at the fish. "No. I caught it."

"But it's suffering!"

Frank shrugged his shoulders. "That's what happens when you catch fish."

"But it's hurting!" Tears welled up.

"It'll die soon."

I turned and ran toward the shack, crying, heartbroken to see the fish suffer.

Mom sympathized with my sadness. When I calmed down, she got a sparkle in her eyes. "I know something that would be fun for you," she said. "Have I ever told you about the wheel and T my brother and I used to play with?"

"No."

"Hm-m-m. Let's go see if we can find the parts to make it for you." She stepped outside the shack, carrying Hazel. I followed. Spotting Dad near the animal pen, we headed that direction. "We need two pieces of wood and a small tire," Mom said.

"For what?"

"A wheel and T for Helen. This pavement would be a perfect place to use it."

"Let me see what I can do," Dad said.

I was intrigued. *What was he making?* I played with Hazel for awhile, then Dad came across the pavement carrying a tire about the size of a lawnmower tire and two pieces of lath board—a long piece and a short piece. He went to the shack. "Are these about right?"

"Perfect," Mom said.

He nailed the short board across the end of the long one to form a T. He handed it to Mom. "You can show her how it works."

Mom stepped out of the shack. She stood the tire on the pavement, then put the T low against the back edge of the tire and began to push. The wheel wobbled over bumps in the pavement. It stayed upright and rolling as she pushed from behind. As she moved the T slightly, putting more pressure on one edge, the wheel turned. She rolled it right to me. "Wow! It's been a long time since I've done that!" She grinned. Handing the T to me, she said, "The point is to keep it rolling. See how long you can keep it up."

I took the T stick and pushed it against the wheel. In short order, the wheel fell over, but I set it back up and tried again . . . and again . . . and again. Hazel laughed and clapped her hands. The wheel and T turned out to be fun for me and entertainment for her.

Between the fun and the work on the farm, in the garden, and feeding the family, by the end of most days, we each fell into bed, and slept well. Others joked about how hard I slept.

I slept so soundly, that one morning, even with eyes still closed, I knew something was different. It was too light. I opened my eyes. Above me was blue sky and sunshine.

I rubbed my eyes. Opened them again. There was still no tent. I turned my head. There were no blanket dividers between "rooms." Our beds just sat there under the sun. The chest of drawers Emma and I shared lay on its front.

I sat up and looked around. Tumbleweeds raced across the pavement and the landscape. A pile of them rested on the side of the pickup. A bank of tumbleweeds on the west side of the shack reached to the roof. As I watched, more tumbleweeds bounced up the wall of weeds, blasted over the shack roof, and flew toward the morning sun. The sheep and goats huddled together in their pen. Emma gathered blanket dividers off the ground to the northeast of our beds. Frank walked around like he was looking for something.

Mom sat on her bed, dressing Hazel.

"Mom," I hollered, "where's the tent?"

She turned toward me, a sad look in her eyes. "A bad windstorm came up," she answered, her voice tense. "A really strong gust tore the tent to shreds."

A few pieces of canvas flew from the poles around our beds.

I spotted Dad walking west, his steps slow . . . almost as if it was hard to put one leg in front of the other. *Where's he going?* I wondered. An instant later, a thought burst into my mind. *The field. If the wind tore our tent to shreds, what did it do to the field?*

CHAPTER 8

Aftermath

My dolls weren't broken, just sprawled on the pavement. Emma and I stood up our chest of drawers.

When I headed to the shack that morning, Dad was still gone. Mom cooked oatmeal.

"Breakfast ready?" Frank asked.

"Dad should be back shortly," Mom answered. Her voice sounded tired. Every now and again, she looked out the door in the direction Dad had gone.

"I'll go look for my plane some more," Frank said and headed out the door.

Emma came in with a bucket of milk. Mom strained it into a jar and placed it in the refrigerator behind what was left of yesterday's milk. She filled a water pitcher from a ten-gallon can outside the door. She took the wash pan outside, poured the used water by garden plants, and refilled the pan. She kept glancing west toward the field. Finally, she set the table, stirred the oatmeal, and set Hazel in her highchair.

Frank came back after a while. "Can't find my plane anyplace," he muttered.

"Maybe you'll find it yet," Mom encouraged.

"But I've already looked everywhere!" He shook his head. "The balsa wood is so light, it may have blown to Idaho." He paused. "I worked so hard cutting out the pieces, building it, painting it, getting every piece just right."

Mom placed a hand on his shoulder and smiled. "And you did a really good job."

"I think it's gone forever," Frank said. His shoulders drooped. "Can we eat yet?"

Mom looked out the door to the west again.

"I'm starved!" Frank wailed.

"Let's go ahead," Mom said.

The rest of us were nearly finished eating when Dad came back. Mom's eyes met his—hers were full of question, his looked sad. "The crop's nearly gone," he said. "The wind whipped the sand. Cut the blades of oat grass off nearly to the ground." He washed his hands in the wash pan and sat down at the table. He grabbed the worship book. "You kids are done eating. We'll read this now."

He read, but not like usual. His voice was monotone. As soon as he finished, we kids started to scatter—it was too sad to stay.

"Frank," Dad called.

Frank turned back.

"I started the pump and set the sprinkler," Dad said. "Would you go out to the field and move it? If there's any chance of any of the oats surviving, we're going to have to keep the sand damp. So, every hour, would you move the sprinkler?"

"Sure," Frank responded. He headed west toward the field . . . passing the animal pen. He stopped at the fence and glared at the ram. He leaned over the fence and banged on it. "I'm going to get you!" he bellowed in the gruffest tone he could muster.

Frank seemed to delight in pestering . . . anyone or anything that would react.

The ram returned the glare. He reared back, then ran toward Frank.

Frank jumped back. The ram slammed into the wooden fence. Frank laughed and headed on toward the field. The ram shook his head and glared at his disappearing target.

Mom came out the door. "Emma?"

"Yeah?"

"The sprinkler's busy in the field today, but the garden plants look pretty pitiful. We've got to get water on them. Would you please take a bucket and carry water from the canal? Pour a little gently down the rows of what's left of the plants."

Emma got the bucket we used to carry water to the animals and headed for the canal.

Hazel became my charge again. We sat on the pavement in the shade of the shack. I stacked blocks. Hazel knocked them down and giggled. I rolled a ball to her. She squealed and hit it in various directions. We watched Emma pour water on the garden plants. I looked where the tent used to be. It looked odd to have beds and dressers sitting in the middle of the pavement under blue sky.

Late morning became moving time. In the shack, Mom scooted the table and chairs closer together. Dad and Frank stacked one chest of drawers on top of the other, just inside the door to the left. We each got one drawer for our clothes and treasures. Bottom drawer was for towels and washcloths. Since I was the shortest, I got the next drawer up.

Then Dad, Mom, Emma, and Frank carried the beds across the pavement. I kept Hazel out of the way of moving feet and furniture. They placed Dad and Mom's bed on the north end of the shack, Frank's on the east side, and Emma's and mine on the west side. The head of each bed was next to the shack.

"Put the crib inside," Mom directed. She squeezed table and chairs closer to the dressers and pointed to the far end of the shack. "Right there, by the window. It's right over the head of our bed, so we can open the window and hear Hazel if she cries."

Over lunch, Paul Harvey's voice was calming. The local news mentioned the previous night's wind, then went on to tell of the booming area economy. Besides the railroad providing stable jobs, construction of the railroad hump yard in Pasco continued—a $5.5 million project.

"That's a funny name," I said. "What's a hump yard?"

"Let's listen to rest of the news," Dad said. "Then we'll talk about it."

The news talked about expansion at Hanford requiring more workers. Construction of McNary Dam near Umatilla, Oregon continued, even though the reservoir behind it was already rising. Building the Umatilla–Plymouth bridge across the Columbia River provided jobs. About thirty-five miles away, the Tri-Cities—Pasco, Kennewick, and Richland—were the nearest towns to Umatilla that could provide major housing and shopping for construction workers and families. And, although it was nearing completion, the new bridge between Pasco and Kennewick still provided jobs.

After the news, Dad sighed. "Wish farming was faring as well as construction!" he said.

"With all that construction," Frank started, "are they getting the gravel they need from that big hole over by Sylvester Street?"

"Probably so," Dad answered. "It's a huge gravel pit." Then Dad turned toward me. "You asked about the hump yard, right?"

"Yeah."

"The railroad is putting in more tracks in the railyard on the north edge of Pasco. At the north end of the rail yard, they're building a hump. Who knows, maybe they're getting rock for that from that big gravel pit too. Anyway, an engine will push a train, car by car, up the hump. A person will disconnect one or several cars, depending on where they're headed. Another person will electronically set which track those cars need to roll onto. So all the goods that need to be shipped to Portland will go on one track. If they need to go to Seattle, they'll go on a different track. And so on."

"So . . . it'll make their work faster?"

"Yep. That'll save the railroad money and help them ship things more quickly."

"Hm-m-m. How's it work?"

"How about we go, after it's built, and watch them work it?"

"Okay."

With all the talk of progress, Frank asked about ours. "So, when are we going to build a house?"

"Wish I knew," Dad said. "Time will tell."

Question was written all over Frank's face. "So . . . if we're still sleeping outside, what are we going to do when it rains?"

Dad glanced at Frank but didn't say a word. Dad looked exhausted . . . defeated.

Mom, with her usual optimism, came to the rescue. "We don't have all the answers yet, Son," she said, "but we'll figure it out."

That night, the cool breeze on my face felt good. Instead of closing my eyes and drifting off to sleep, I looked up at the Milky Way glittering across the sky. Going to bed under the stars was a new experience. *How far to the stars?* I wondered. *And when will rain come?*

CHAPTER 9

Burst of Beauty

T he next morning there was no rain in sight. Day after sweltering day passed. The sun beat down. Emma or Frank kept moving the sprinkler, watering the whole field. Slowly some plants grew again. The oats didn't come back very strong, but there was at least some green in the field. The garden didn't fare much better, but we still watered it and pulled a few small radishes and carrots from the sand.

In July, my job got harder—Hazel took her first steps. Before long, we had to watch her even more carefully than before because she could walk toward the canal a lot faster than she'd been able to crawl.

Garden crops began to mature. We picked string beans. I snapped mounds of them into pieces. At mealtime, they tasted great. What we didn't eat fresh, Mom canned in quart jars.

As July wound down, the local news centered on the opening of the new bridge. July 30, the radio talked about the crowd of three thousand people waiting for the dedication ceremony. Water skiers and music entertained them. A motorcade of dignitaries, set to be the first to cross the new bridge, waited in their cars on the Pasco side of the river. At 11:40, two officials cut the ribbon.

Over the radio, we heard engines start. "What?" the radio announcer exploded. "Bicycles! Several boys on bicycles just raced past the motorcade! They're headed up the bridge . . . up and over the bridge! The first to cross the new bridge were boys on bicycles!"

We laughed. "Those boys," Mom said, "will remember that for a good long time!"

The rest of the festivities proceeded as planned. One of the first Tri-Citians to cross had also been one of the first people to cross the old bridge when it was dedicated thirty-two years earlier in 1922.

Next time we went to town, Frank suggested, "Hey, let's drive across the new bridge!" And Dad did. It just seemed like the thing to do.

One August evening at supper, Dad said, "I've got some good news and some bad news. Let's get the bad news out of the way first."

Emma looked sidelong at him like she'd heard enough bad news for a lifetime. We all eyed him.

"I called the real estate agent again today. There's still no one interested in buying our 160 acres of hillsides in Oregon."

Emma and Frank both groaned.

"So," Dad went on, "unless something else comes up pretty soon, we're apt to have a tough winter." He let that settle in the silence for a long minute. "Anyone want the good news?"

"Yes!"

"The peaches are ripe at Ringold Farms," Dad continued, "and they're hiring pickers."

The next morning after chores, breakfast, and making sack lunches, Emma, Frank, and I piled into the bed of the pickup, while Dad, Mom, and Hazel rode in the cab. Late that afternoon, we came home with some cash and three large boxes of peaches. As soon as we arrived home, Dad headed to the field to restart the water. Fresh peaches for supper tasted wonderful.

The next morning, Dad, Emma, and Frank headed out again, but Mom, Hazel, and I stayed home. "We've got work to do," Mom explained. "I need you to help me can peaches."

Mom washed boxes of quart canning jars, then scalded a dishpan full of peaches.

"How come you're dunking the peaches in boiling water?" I asked.

"So they'll be easy to peel," Mom said. "You'll see how the peeling slips right off."

She was right. Between our watching Hazel, I slid the skin off peaches and Mom halved them and filled jar after jar. When seven were filled, she added sugar and water, screwed the scalded lids as tightly as possible, and submerged the jars in the large canning kettle. While the water heated, I kept peeling peaches and she filled more jars. After twenty-five minutes of boiling, Mom carefully applied a jar lifter around the glass throat of the jar so she wouldn't touch the metal lids. She set one jar after another on the counter. After a few minutes, I heard a pop. "What was that?"

"Just a jar sealing," Mom answered. Pointing to the hot jars, she said, "See how the lids are all bulged up except for this one?"

"Yeah."

Just then another pop. Suddenly another lid curved slightly down rather than up.

"When they pop like that, they seal," Mom explained. "That means they won't spoil. We can save them and enjoy them this winter."

The pops continued until all seven jars had sealed. I kept watching Hazel and peeling peaches. Mom kept scalding peaches, cutting them, filling jars, scalding lids in a small kettle, putting jars in the large canning kettle, timing the boiling, and taking the jars out. A large burner on the electric range was red hot constantly. Even with both shack windows and the door open, no breeze wafted the steam away—the one day we needed wind to cool us off and there wasn't a breath of a breeze! Sweat poured down our faces.

As the day progressed, the counter filled with jars of golden peaches preserved for winter use.

That night, the peach pickers arrived home with more cash, more peaches, and Frank tormenting Emma. "I picked more peaches than you did!"

"Sure," Emma retorted. "Three more?"

"No, a whole box more."

"But that last box was tiny!"

"No, it . . ."

"Hey, you honyocks," Dad interrupted. "Frank, you have more energy than you know what to do with. Go change the water in the field."

Frank headed toward the field sing-songing, "I picked more peaches! I picked more peaches."

Emma shook her head. "Sometimes I want to sock him in the stomach again."

"Again?" I asked. "Did you hit him?"

"Yeah, a long time ago," she said. "I was minding my own business—just trying to read the newspaper. He kept poking the paper . . . over . . . and over . . . and over again. I finally threw down the newspaper, jumped up, and socked him a good one in the stomach." She grinned. "He turned white as a sheet and went and lay down." Emma laughed. "He didn't bug me for several days."

"Did you get in trouble?" I asked.

"No," Emma said. "I didn't. You know Mom has eyes in the back of her head. She saw the whole thing and just left well enough alone."

I glanced at Mom. She just grinned and kept preparing supper.

We had fresh peaches for supper dessert and for breakfast fruit the next morning. When the pickers went off to work that day, Mom and I set to canning peaches all over again. By the time peach season was over, we'd earned some cash, enjoyed lots of fresh peaches, and stored over a hundred quarts of golden fruit on the floor under the counter and shelves.

One afternoon, Dad sat with a funny-looking piece of equipment. He rubbed a small round thing against its curved edge. "What's that?" I asked.

"A scythe," Dad replied. "It's for cutting the oats."

"What are you doing?"

He held up the round, gray thing in his right hand. "This is a whet stone," he said. "I'm sharpening the scythe so it will cut well."

After breakfast and worship the next morning, Dad announced, "Time to harvest what oats we have." Then he added, "At least we'll have some food for the livestock."

Mom's Adam's apple squiggled like she swallowed hard.

"But I think we'd better sell some of the lambs." Dad looked at Frank. "We're not going to have a lot of crop. Selling some lambs would give us a little cash and save on animal food through the winter."

"Can we keep the ewe lambs?" Frank asked. "So we can grow the herd? And have more wool to sell?"

"How about if we sell the rams and about half the ewes?" Dad asked.

"Just the lambs?"

"Yep, I'm just talking about the lambs," Dad said. "We need the adult ram so we have lambs next year."

Frank agreed.

"We'll get in what oats we have," Dad continued. "And if the animals have food this winter, we'll have milk." He took a breath, then said, "Emma and Frank, you each get a pitchfork and come with me." Dad got the scythe and the three headed toward the field.

Hazel and I followed shortly to see what was going on. Dad swung the sharp blade of the scythe near the ground. Where the scythe swung, the oat grass fell flat on the ground. Frank watched for a while, then Dad handed him the scythe. Emma pitchforked the oats into piles. On through the field they went—swinging, cutting, raking up the hay with the pitchfork, then lifting it into one pile after another.

Later, they pitchforked the piles into the pickup bed, hauled the load near the livestock pens, and scraped the oat grass onto the pavement. When all the oats had been harvested and piled near the animals, Dad and Frank covered the stack with a large canvas tarp.

One afternoon as Hazel napped, I wandered northeast of the shack, head down, watching to avoid cactus spines in my ankles— even the cacti didn't grow very tall. Nor did I care to step on a horned toad, or run into a black widow spider or rattlesnake. I meandered aimlessly for some time, wishing Smokey was bounding along beside me.

Suddenly color caught my eye. I stopped. There, to my left, just inches above the desert floor, deep blue blossoms stretched toward the sun. I knelt, examining my find.

A cluster of three small blossoms, as deep a blue as royal robes, stretched from one short stem. A spot of gold hid in the deepest recess of the bowl of each flower. The throat shone purple, as deep and rich a color as the blue it melded into.

I leaned closer, marveling at the burst of beauty. The flowers were the most beautiful thing I'd seen since we moved away from our woods. I squatted there, drinking in the rich color. As I gazed at the gorgeous flower, the friends and family we'd left behind, our tent, and our shack kitchen faded from focus. The rare beauty seemed to lift me from dreariness.

Eventually, I stood again. Loathe to leave, I continued to admire the flowers. As suddenly as the color had caught my eye, a thought welled up in my heart: *There's beauty everywhere. Some places you just have to look a lot harder.*

CHAPTER 10

Cooling

As summer droned on, I occasionally overheard Mom and Dad talking about school. "How are we going to pay for school?"

"I don't know, but surely something will work out."

"But private school takes money and we don't have much of that."

"Keep praying. Something will work out."

When the August day for school registration arrived, we bathed in the irrigation canal, dressed in our best, and went to town.

First, Dad and Mom talked with the principal—Dale's dad was both teacher and principal. "We want our children to have a Christian education," Dad said, "and we're willing to do whatever we can, but this has been a really tough year. Is there anything we can do to make it possible for our three children to attend?"

The principal asked questions, puzzled a bit, then said, "I'm not sure what, but go ahead and register your children for school. The school board meets tonight. We'll see what we can do. Can you call me tomorrow?"

The teacher of first and second grades wanted to put me in first grade.

"She didn't go to a school last year because it was too far for her to walk," Mom explained. "But I went through the books with her. She's ready for second grade."

"That's fine," the teacher replied, "but I've found that often that doesn't work out too well."

My quiet, kind Mom swallowed. "Ma'am, she is advanced beyond first grade material," she insisted. "How about if you try her in second grade. If she can't do the work, then we'll agree for you to move her back to first grade."

So, I was registered for second grade. Emma and Frank were both registered for ninth grade.

The next day, Dad drove to the telephone booth at Matthew's Corner. When he came home, he was all smiles. "The principal asked, 'Would you folks be willing to work?' I said, 'Yes! Of course!' He said, 'The church needs a janitor. If your family would be willing to clean the church, the church will pay the school directly, and your three young people can attend school.'" Dad looked at the three of us kids. "So, you honyocks, would you be willing to help clean the church week after week?"

"When do we start?" Frank asked.

"Next week." Dad turned toward Mom. "Can we make Thursday afternoons the time?"

"Sure," Mom said. "I see no reason why Thursday afternoons won't work."

The next week the previous janitor showed us where the vacuum cleaner, brooms, mops, dusting cloths, and various cleaning supplies were kept. He showed us each room that needed to be cleaned and gave Mom keys to the church.

Mom organized us into crews, and we set to work.

A couple weeks later, school started. At first Mom or Dad drove us the twenty miles to school. Then they discovered two other students lived about halfway there. Mom or Dad drove us to the Olsons'[1]* place, and we rode with them. In the afternoon, except for Thursdays, Mom or Dad picked us all up. Frank and the Olson

---

1 Names have been changed.

boys generally rode on a bench in the back of the pickup. With the canopy breaking the wind, they were more comfortable there than crowding onto the pickup seat with the rest of us. We dropped off the two Olson boys at their home on the way to ours.

Frank acted excited about school. His friend, Dale, was there, as well as others he could play softball with. "What's your favorite subject?" Mom asked one evening.

"Recess," Frank replied without hesitation. "Same as it's been all throughout school."

Emma seemed less enthusiastic about school. She didn't complain but never acted excited about it. Whether at school or at home, she generally just quietly did her work.

I enjoyed learning. If the teacher had just let me listen and absorb, I'd have thought school was delightful. But she asked questions, and when it was my turn to read aloud, she usually interrupted me. "I can't hear you," she said. "Speak louder." My bashful voice didn't know how to speak louder.

By mid-September, the radio news talked about the dedication of McNary Dam. The dam was named in honor of Charles McNary, a US senator from Oregon whose legislation had helped make Grand Coulee Dam and Bonneville Dam a reality. Grand Coulee Dam was the one that made irrigated farming in the Columbia Basin possible. Bonneville Dam was nearer Portland, Oregon. Both of these previously built dams generated electricity.

McNary Dam had already impacted the Tri-Cities—its reservoir had raised the water level for sixty-four miles above the dam. It would provide benefits—electrical power and a navigation lock to improve shipping on the river. That would help keep shipping costs lower, so farmers could sell their wheat and other crops at a profit.

Those who planned the dedication ceremony for the dam were especially excited about one scheduled speaker—President of the United States, Dwight Eisenhower.

On September 23, 1954, about thirty thousand people crowded the dam's powerhouse to hear President Eisenhower's speech.

Afterward, he pressed the button which activated the dam's fifth (and last) generator for the first time.

The news, however, was often crowded out by our own chores. The neighbor about a mile north of us had grown pinto beans. After they dried in the field, a bean combine harvested them, but the big machine couldn't get to all the ends and corners. Some bean plants stood undisturbed. Dad discovered them and asked the farmer if we could come pick them.

"Of course you can," the neighbor assured him. "We're done in the field. Glean all the beans you want."

After school, we took buckets and bags. "Pick to your heart's content," Dad said. We picked beans way beyond where my heart was content.

Finally, suppertime came. We happily quit picking beans and descended on supper. The next afternoon and the next, we picked dry beans, until we pretty well cleaned up the field, After we drove home each day, we dumped the beans on the pavement, took off our shoes, and walked around on the pile. Beans popped out of their dry shells.

"Do you realize," Frank taunted, "that you're walking in your food?"

"We'll wash them," Emma replied.

"Still, you've got your stinky feet in your supper!" Frank persisted.

Emma gave him the evil-eye glare that usually ended his teasing . . . for the moment.

We raked up some of the shells and stems. The breeze blew away the chaff. Then we gathered the beans off the pavement and dumped them in large burlap bags.

"You'll be glad this winter for the gunnysacks of beans," Mom assured us.

By the end of September, the air changed. Nights became chilly. Inside the shack, Dad added six nails on the wall between the dressers and table—a nail for a coat for each of us. Outside, we added quilts to all the beds. Mom dragged out flannel nightgowns from someplace and Emma and I were glad for them. In the morning

I changed clothes under the covers, folded my nightgown, placed it neatly under my pillow, and lay in bed, dreading to get out in the cold.

"Up and at 'em," Dad hollered.

I jumped up, threw my side of the covers over my pillow, tidied it a bit, raced toward the shack door, and threw it open. "Br-r-r," I shivered one morning.

"Good morning!" Mom greeted with her usual smile and lilt in her voice. "Come get warm."

By the time she finished speaking, I'd slammed the door behind me and leaned over the oven door. The electric oven and range-top burners provided the only heat for the shack. Fortunately for us kids, Mom was always up early and had the oven heating.

"When are we going to get a house?" I asked.

Mom's smile disappeared. "I don't know." She swallowed. "Our house in Oregon hasn't sold yet and we hardly got any crops. We barely have money to buy groceries and pay the electric bill. We don't have money to build a house."

"But it's getting cold," I wailed.

"Yes, it is," she agreed. Her lips spread into a small smile. "But, somehow, everything's going to work out."

Once I warmed a bit, I ran to the outhouse, did my job as quickly as nature allowed, and rushed back inside. Racing one way or the other, I often noticed Emma or Frank milking. I began to be thankful I wasn't big enough to do some jobs!

"Is our house in Oregon ever going to sell?" Frank asked over breakfast. "Are we ever going to get to sleep in a warm place again?"

"Yeah, next summer when it's 102," Emma quipped.

"No!" Frank objected. "In a house where we can be warm even in winter!"

Dad sighed. "I hope it won't be too long," he said. "But I can't tell you when."

In October, Mom started adding a little hot water from the tea-kettle to the wash pan to break the chill of morning face washing. At breakfast, I often held my hands against the outside of my bowl of mush—what some people call hot cereal. The warmth felt good. It also felt good having something warm in my belly.

One morning after Dad listened to the weather forecast, he asked Mom, "Do we have any more blankets? Sounds like there's going to be frost on the pumpkin soon."

"Not here," Mom said, then added with an impish grin, "The pumpkins I planted didn't grow."

Kidding aside, that day Mom added all the rest of the blankets and quilts to our beds, and Dad found canvas to cover each. The canvas came just in time—rain fell, but the canvas kept the moisture from soaking into our bedding. Unfortunately, it didn't keep the air from feeling cold when I finally had to crawl out of bed to make it in time for breakfast!

With November, white frost often covered the canvas on our beds first thing in the morning. Br-r-r-r. It was cold in bed. It was colder to get up. But we all braved the cold and showed up for breakfast.

One afternoon, Hazel and I watched as the rest took the canopy off the pickup and placed it over Frank's single bed. He got the luxury suite—he had walls and a roof. Emma and I got an upgrade, too—Dad brought long 2-inch by 10-inch planks. He and Frank laid one end of a board against the roof of the shack, the other end on the ground at the foot of our bed. They added and fastened several more until the planks barely covered the bed's width.

Dad stood back and looked at the makeshift lean-to. "Mission accomplished," he said. He started to gather up his tools.

"What are you going to put over your bed?" Emma asked.

"We don't really have anything else," Dad said.

"Nothing?"

"We have the canvas on our bed."

"Aren't there some more boards?"

"If there were more boards," Dad said, "we'd make your covering wider. But there aren't any more."

Frank laughed. "If the rain or snow comes *straight* down, it won't get you wet," he quipped.

I shivered. "Snow?"

CHAPTER 11

Thanksgiving

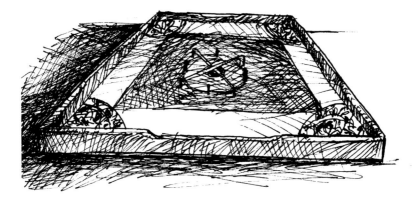

I ce began forming overnight on top of the water in the milk cans. We would have been delighted to have some of the luke-warm water that resulted from summer sun. Instead, someone had to break through the ice before we could pour water.

Whatever the temperature or season, Frank or Emma hauled buckets of water from the canal for the animals. They often had to break the ice on top of the animals' tubs of drinking water. They pulled oats out from under the canvas to feed the creatures. Sometimes Frank milked and Emma fed the critters, sometimes vice versa. The sheep with their woolly coats were the fortunate ones in winter. The ram and billy goat had grown bigger—they still butted heads, and the thudding was louder. Maybe they kept up the duel-ing to keep warm.

Laundry still needed to be washed and there wasn't room for the washing machine and tub inside the shack. The water cooled down faster than in summer. Mom kept adding hot water to warm it up. She or Emma would come in the shack after hanging one load of laundry and warm their hands at the open oven door. The clothes on the line froze stiff. It took several days of freezing and thawing for the sun to finally dry them.

If someone caught a cold, Mom boiled a kettle of water and added a few drops of eucalyptus oil to it. She made a tent out of a blanket to hold the steam in and had the congested person sit under it and breathe the steam. When I was the patient, with one or a few treatments, I either was well or desperately wished I was.

Sore throat? Mom wet a cotton sock . . . with *cold* water. She wrapped it around my neck and covered it by wrapping a dry wool sock around it and safety pinning it in place. Then she sent me out into the cold night to crawl into my cold bed. By morning the cotton sock was warm and my throat usually felt fine, or at least much better. (The cold outside and cold bed were not part of the treatment—just part of our reality.)

The treatment if we scraped or cut ourselves made us shudder—iodine. It stung like all get out! It hurt worse than the hurt! It was awfully tempting to try to hide any injury. But it apparently worked well, because with all the scrapes and scratches four kids could come up with on a farm, not one of our injuries ever got infected.

Cod liver oil was supposed to be good for us. We each got a teaspoonful every morning with breakfast. One morning when Mom held out a spoonful of the nasty tasting liquid toward me, I courteously said, "No, thank you."

Dad didn't miss a beat. "Sorry, kiddo. No cod liver oil, no breakfast."

I looked at Dad, at Mom, at the spoonful of nasty tasting liquid she still held out toward me. I looked at my empty bowl. My stomach growled. I opened my mouth. As usual, as soon as I swallowed the oily liquid, I wolfed down several swallows of milk, trying to wash down the taste.

To keep clean, we took "spit baths." We each had our own washcloth. We'd pour warm water from the teakettle onto it, rub soap onto it, and wash. Then we rinsed the soap out of our washcloth in the hand-washing pan, wrung it, and wiped off the soap.

Once a week we took real baths. On warm days (a relative term), we went to the canal. But when the temperature stayed below freezing, Mom took pity on those of us who didn't want to break ice on our bath water.

"Sissies!" Frank called as he headed to the canal, soap, towel, and washcloth in hand.

Mom heated water on the kitchen range. We filled the metal washtub and folded into it. I was fortunate to be near the youngest—only second in line for the bath water.

Sometimes it was cold enough that even Frank opted for the weekly indoor bath. "Sissy!" one of us girls taunted.

He grinned. "It's cold out there!"

To warm up, we hovered around the open oven door, coattails held out, trying to catch all the heat we could. The oven, along with six bodies in the small space, usually warmed up the shack eventually.

With colder temperatures, came shorter days and longer nights. After Emma and Frank had their homework done, Dad would often read aloud to us—especially on Friday evenings. He didn't read in a monotone voice that would put us to sleep. Oh, no. He made learning fun. He read with expression that kept us saying, "One more chapter? Ple-e-ease?"

He read biographies to us—books about people like Abraham Lincoln, David Livingstone, George Washington Carver. He read stories about various places around the world—Australia, Africa, South America. He read books about animals, about nature—Sam Campbell's books about the woods and wildlife near his family's summer cabin on a wooded Wisconsin island were favorites. I didn't just hear Dad reading. In my mind, I saw twin fawns Fiddlesticks and Freckles frolicking in the woods, laughed at Salt and Pepper's porcupine antics, experienced Eeny, Meeny, Miney, Mo, and Still-Mo rollicking in raccoon-style.

Dad learned early to appreciate stories. His mom had a friend in high school who later traveled the world. She wrote numerous books about exciting experiences, and she also wrote letters to her friend. When a letter from Norma Youngberg arrived, Grandmommy would gather her eager children around her rocking chair and read the letter to them. Dad still read every one of her books he could get his hands on. And he read them to us.

When Thanksgiving Day came, the goats were milked as usual. Right after breakfast, while most of us still sat at the table, Mom started dinner preparation.

"Are you cooking a turkey?" Frank asked.

"No."

"But Papa always caught a turkey on Thanksgiving and Grandmommy always cooked it for our special dinner."

Mom turned toward Frank. "You're missing Papa and Grandmommy, aren't you?"

"Yeah. We always went there for Thanksgiving. And the house was full of aunts and uncles and cousins. And we haven't gotten to see any of them for months."

"And full of Grandmommy's beautiful paintings too," Emma added.

"Yes," Mom said. "The house was always beautiful, and warm, and welcoming. And it has been a long time."

"Will Grandmommy be able to cook Thanksgiving dinner this year?" Emma asked.

"No. Others are doing the cooking this year. They're getting together at Papa and Grandmommy's place, but others are providing the meal."

Dad's cheeks turned red and his eyes got moist. He pulled his red handkerchief out of his overalls pocket and blew his nose.

"I'm sure there'll be plenty of food," Mom said. "There are other good cooks too, but your Aunt Verda always brings enough single-handedly to feed an army."

"When will we get to see them all?" Frank asked.

"I don't know, Son." Mom looked over at Dad.

"I don't know either," Dad said. His voice quivered. He wiped his nose again. "As you know, our crops didn't turn out very well this year. So we don't have money for making trips."

Frank nodded. "I know."

"I hope farming here will be more successful next year," Dad added.

Hazel banged her spoon on her highchair tray.

Mom, working at the counter, turned. "Frank," she said. "I'd like to make buns for our dinner, but I've got a lot to do. Would you grind some wheat for me?" She held the hand grinder out to him.

"Sure, Mom." He took the grinder and fastened it to the table. Mom handed him a bag of wheat. He poured wheat in the top, turned the handle, and soon had flour enough for bread.

Emma and I looked over pinto beans to be sure no shells, stones, or pieces of pavement were mixed in. "Keep your feet out of them!" Frank advised.

We each gave him a dirty look and he grinned.

Besides baking bread that morning, we cooked pinto beans till they were tender, baked squash, and boiled a quart of string beans. And Mom baked a pumpkin pie—we called it pumpkin pie, but she made it out of winter squash.

"Your pie sure is good!" Frank enthused. "The only thing that could make it better is if it had whipped cream on top."

Dad drew in a deep breath, then sighed. "Maybe someday we can get a cow—a cow that gives plenty of milk and the milk has a good head of cream."

After dinner, a cold wind blew outside. We hunkered in the shack.

"Let's play Crokinole!" Frank suggested.

"Yeah!" came a chorus.

Frank pulled the Crokinole board out from behind Hazel's crib. The game board had once belonged to Dad's grandpa. Dad had played many a game with his grandpa and various cousins before the worn board came to live with our family. We thumped the same disks his grandpa had once thumped into the middle 20-point depression.

Dad spoke of his grandpa with such respect that it seemed like a privilege to play his favorite game. Besides, it was fun.

The goal of the game was to get to 100 points. The board had four concentric rings—a tiny depression in the middle, then three other circles, each one larger than the last. At the end of each round, each disk in the outside circle was worth 5 points, in the next circle worth 10 points, in the smallest ring 15 points, and in the middle depression 20 points. The board also had equally spaced pegs to increase the challenge.

The playing pieces were wooden rings about an inch across—one person or team played with twelve red rings, the other with green. If the opposition had a ring on the board, the current shooter had to aim to knock it off. He also tried to aim so that when he knocked the opponent's ring off the board, his own would stay in the highest-point area possible. Best of all was if your ring would land in the 20-point depression in the center. Anytime that happened, 20 points was added to your score immediately. All others were counted only after all 12 rings from each side were played.

Since I was the youngest and least proficient, when I played, I got to be on the same team as the highest-scoring player. That pretty well evened things out—or put the high scorer at a disadvantage. Whoever's turn, the position of the disk took precision planning and each thump took total focus.

"You'll never make it!" Frank insisted when Emma aimed at one of his rings. "Can't do it!"

"Oh, hush," Emma responded.

"You may as well give up. You know I'll beat you."

Emma gave him her evil-eye glare. It didn't do any good. After a few more taunts, she glared at him, then snapped, "Want me to slug you in the stomach?"

He backed off, but the smirk didn't leave his expression.

The game needed either two or four players, so either one or three of us would sit out a game and keep Hazel entertained. If I was playing with Hazel at the other end of the shack and couldn't see where a disk careened on the board, I still had a pretty good idea of its success by the excited, "Yeah!" or the descending "Ugh" of the shooter.

Eventually we chose other games—Sorry, Pick-Up-Sticks, or Dominoes. We played the afternoon away. The shack was filled with happy banter. The hoots and hollers made happy bedlam.

Dad and Frank did the evening animal chores while Mom and Emma popped popcorn and got out home-canned peaches. It truly felt like a holiday!

"It's been a fun day!" Mom exclaimed.

"And it's warm in here!" Frank added.

Emma shuddered. "I hate the thought of going outside and crawling into a cold bed!"

CHAPTER 12

Rich

T hen it was December. At school the teacher talked about a Christmas program. She told us we would each play a part in front of all our family and friends. My heart beat faster. I didn't have any interest in standing in front of a bunch of people whispering a part that no one could hear.

When she got through handing out parts, she hadn't given me one—she must have realized my bashful voice would ruin the play. I started to relax. Then came fateful words. "Helen, I'm going to give you a poem to recite." My heart started pounding in my throat. "It's a long poem by Henry Wadsworth Longfellow, but I'm just going to give you three stanzas. I know you can learn it."

At the end of that school day, the teacher reminded us, "Everyone take your part home and learn your lines."

I gave the poem to Mom. "I don't want to say a poem in front of a bunch of people."

She smiled knowingly. "For now, just learn it," she said. "I'll help you learn how to say it."

So, I started memorizing the poem.

A few days later, a big fir tree stood in the corner of our classroom. *Where'd they get a Christmas tree,* I wondered.

I thought about how we got our Christmas tree when we lived in our wooded wonderland. Our whole family bundled up with snow pants, boots, and our warmest coats, hats, and mittens. We trudged through the snowy woods, Dad carrying a saw. Emma and Frank plowed ahead—their legs were longer than mine. "Here's a tree!" one would yell.

"That one's too big to fit in the house."

"How about this one?"

"Too bare."

"This one?"

"Let's look some more."

Eventually we all agreed on a tree. Dad or Frank cut it down, and we took turns dragging it to the house. After we unbundled, Mom got out red, green, and yellow construction paper. We cut strips, made paper chains, and strung them around the Christmas tree. Then Mom popped popcorn and got needles and thread. We strung cranberries and popcorn—except for the puffy pieces of popcorn we ate—and wound the red and white strings around the tree. We hung colorful balls and shiny, silver tinsel on branches, then topped the tree with a cardboard star covered with shiny aluminum foil. Getting the tree and decorating it was an all-day event of fun and delight.

But that was memory. This would be our first Christmas in the desert. At school we also made construction paper loops and chains and decorated the classroom tree.

At home, Mom worked with me on my poem. "Stand straight and tall."

I forced my spine straight and shoulders back.

"What's the first line?"

"I heard the bells on Christmas day," I quoted.

"No," Mom said.

"Yes, that's the first line," I protested.

"Yes, I know it is. But stop and think." She paused and got a gleam in her eye. "What do bells sound like?" she asked. "How do you feel when you hear bells ring?"

"Hm-m-m. Bells make me happy."

"Yes. Kind of excited?"

"Yeah."

"Then imagine . . ." Her voice held quiet excitement. "Imagine you really hear bells." She paused, then spoke slowly and distinctly. "Say that first line . . . as if you were hearing bells ring."

I closed my eyes and imagined bells. I smiled and opened my eyes. "I heard the bells," I said, "on Christmas day." There was a lilt in my voice that hadn't been there before.

"So much better!" Mom praised. "Think about the words of every line . . . and say them like you were right there listening to the bells."

We went over each line, each word—so I knew what they meant. That afternoon I reread the poem and thought about how to say each line.

The next afternoon Mom showed me how to speak louder. "Now," she said, "go just outside the shack and speak your poem so the sheep and goats can hear."

"I could go closer so I don't have to talk so loud," I said.

"No, no," Mom said. "When you say your poem at the program, you need to speak loudly and clearly so the people in the very back row can hear you." She smiled. "Whatever you do, always do your very best!"

So I stood at the corner of the shack and started, "I heard the bells on Christmas day . . ."

The sheep and goats looked up at me. They must have heard.

". . . Their old familiar carols play . . ."

Days passed. By the time I was through practicing, the goats and sheep probably knew my lines. And Mom smiled. "You're doing a good job!" she praised.

The evening of the program, I was quiet as we drove to school. Frank and Emma chattered about their pieces in the upper-grade part of the program. When we arrived, Mom turned me toward her and put a hand on each of my shoulders. She smiled. "You don't need to be nervous, Helen," she said. "You know your poem very well. Don't worry about all the people out in front of you. Just say your poem with the expression you've been practicing. Say it loudly and clearly just like you've been doing every day." She grinned. "Say it so the sheep and goats can hear you."

When our class's play finished and the applause quieted, I climbed the steps to the platform and walked to the center. I looked at Mom. She smiled. In my mind I heard her say, *Whatever you do, always do your best.* I took a deep breath, straightened to my full height, thrust my shoulders back, and spoke:

> I heard the bells on Christmas Day
> Their old familiar carols play . . .

My teacher gasped. Her eyes opened wide.

Had I done something wrong? I was sure I'd said the words correctly. And I'd said them with expression like Mom had taught me. And I'd said them so the sheep and goats could've heard and understood each word if they'd been sitting in the very back row. Not knowing what else to do, I continued:

> And wild and sweet
> The words repeat
> Of peace on earth, good-will to men! . . .

The applause was loud when I finished all three stanzas. I caught Mom's eye—she smiled broadly and looked proud as pie. I curtsied as I'd been taught. I stepped off the platform and walked down the side aisle. My teacher leaned over and looked me straight in the eye. "You did a bea-u-tiful job!"

Just one problem—now she knew I could speak above a whisper.

On the way home, Frank asked. "What are we going to do for Christmas?"

Emma snickered. "One thing's sure—we're not going to walk out in the woods and cut down a tree!"

We all laughed. But even though I laughed, I had a sad, empty feeling.

"There's no place in the shack to put a tree anyway," Mom added

"But if we don't have a tree," Frank lamented, "we won't get to put it outside after Christmas and watch the birds come eat the strings of popcorn and cranberries."

"Even if we don't have a tree," Mom said, "we'll do something." She paused. "In fact, Dad and I were talking about that." She cleared her throat. "How about if we go shopping after your last day of school—just as your Christmas vacation starts?"

"We don't have much money this year," Dad added, "but we'll give you each a dollar. You can be thinking about what you want to get with it."

At breakfast the last morning before Christmas break, Mom said, "Did you remember that we'll go Christmas shopping this afternoon?"

Anticipation filled our voices. "Yeah!"

"If you've saved any money, you may want to take it with you this morning," Mom added.

After breakfast Emma and Frank each went to their drawer and pulled out some change from under their clothes. Maybe they'd saved some from picking fruit. But I didn't have any money.

That afternoon after school, as soon as we piled into the pickup, Mom opened her purse. She pulled out three one-dollar bills, handed us each one, and we headed toward Woolworth's—a "five and dime" store that carried a wide selection of inexpensive items.

As Frank tucked his dollar bill into his pocket, he demanded, "When we get to the store, don't follow me around!"

"Right," Mom responded. "Let each other shop without looking at what they're buying. And, Helen, I'll help you. All you have is one dollar. And you want to get a gift for everyone, don't you?"

In the store, Christmas music played—"Silver Bells," "Rudolph the Red-Nosed Reindeer," "Silent Night," and other songs. Mom, holding Hazel, and I wandered up one aisle and down another. We discussed the prices of different items—what I could and couldn't get with my dollar. Back and forth we traipsed. I finally picked up gifts for Hazel, Emma, Frank, and Dad. "How much will I have left?" I asked.

Mom looked at the prices. "Nineteen . . . thirty-four . . . forty-four . . ." I could see she was adding the numbers in her mind. "Fifty-nine cents," she concluded. "You still have forty-one cents."

"Okay," I said. "Now you need to go someplace else."

Mom smiled and wandered to another part of the store.

I went back to the shelf where I'd seen a certain spoon—the spoon was the size of a serving spoon, but it had a long, sturdy handle. Mom worked hard to cook for us. I thought it would be a nice spoon for stirring in deep kettles or dishes. I took my finds to the clerk. The lady smiled. She punched the prices into her cash register. "Good job, young lady," she said. "You get two pennies back." She gave me the two pennies and stuffed all my purchases into a brown paper bag.

Walking out of the store, I felt rich—I had gifts for everyone!

1954–1955

CHAPTER 13

Winter

At home I asked Mom, "Can I wrap my gifts now?"

"Sure," she said. She stopped supper preparation and got out scissors, a couple brown paper bags she'd saved from when she bought groceries, and the ball of string she added to anytime we received a package with string. "Why don't you get your crayons? You may want to draw Christmas pictures on your packages."

I cut paper, wrapped a gift, and wrote "To." "How do you spell Emma?" I asked.

"E."

I wrote it with my red crayon, then followed suit with the other letters.

"M . . . M . . . A."

I barely started to wrap Frank's gift when the door creaked open. I turned—there stood Frank with a bucket of milk.

"Don't look over here!" I yelled. I leaned over his gift, trying to hide it.

"I'm going to look!" he said.

"No!"

"Maybe I'll just come get my gift right now," he taunted.

"No!" I screamed. "Go outside!"

"I'm going to look."

Mom came to my rescue. She grinned at Frank. "You tease!" she exclaimed. "How about you go back outside for just a few minutes. Are the animals fed yet?"

"No," he admitted and headed out the door.

I wrapped his gift as quickly as I could. "How do you spell Frank?" I asked.

"F . . . R . . . A . . . N . . . K." And so it went for Hazel too. I knew how to spell Mom and Dad. And I knew how to spell "From" and my own name. I colored green Christmas trees on each package and crayoned them with red balls. I scooted a chair over to the chests of drawers, stood on the chair, reached up and laid each wrapped gift on top. I was ready for Christmas.

Well, almost ready. That evening while Dad read aloud to us, Emma and I cut strips of red and green construction paper.

"We need a wise men's star," Emma said. She drew a star on yellow construction paper. We hung a paper chain over each window and the star above the east window.

It didn't look as Christmasy as usual—either inside or outside. No trees. And our decorations were in a box somewhere in our house in the forest. But we could think Christmas goodwill in a small shack with just a few decorations.

On Christmas eve when we opened gifts, Mom exclaimed over my gift to her, "What a nice spoon! Thank you, Helen!"

The very next morning Mom used it to stir pancake batter. She looked at me and smiled. "My new spoon stirs very nicely!" she exclaimed. Her eyes smiled too. "I'll use it a lot!"

With Christmas over, life went back to normal—animal chores outside. Inside there were meals to fix, dishes to wash and dry, peace to keep. At night, bounding into cold beds to escape the colder, damper, breezy air.

At supper a couple of days after Christmas, Dad said, "Tomorrow we're going . . ." He choked up, pulled his red handkerchief out of his back overalls' pocket, and wiped his nose. He closed his eyes. His body shook, like with sobs, but there was no sound.

Emma and Frank glanced at each other, then at Mom. She watched Dad.

Finally, Dad broke the uncomfortable silence. "Tomorrow we're going to go see my mom. We'll need to get up early so we can see her fairly early in the day. She feels stronger in the morning."

Later when Mom and Emma were doing dishes, Emma said, "I thought we didn't have money to go to Papa and Grandmommy's. How come we're going?"

"Grandmommy's very ill," Mom said. "It's important that we go now."

The next morning we got up in darkness. Dad and Frank did chores. Mom and Emma made sandwiches for both breakfast and dinner. It was still dark when we climbed into the pickup.

Heading west alongside the Columbia River, my enthusiasm started a sing-song "We're going to Papa and Grandmommy's! We're going to Papa and Grandmommy's!"

"Not exactly," Mom interrupted.

I looked at her with question.

"Grandmommy moved," Mom said. "She's very sick. Papa couldn't take care of her any more. She moved to her sister's house."

"So we're not going to their farm?" I asked.

"No."

"There's a good side to that," Dad added. "It's closer—only 250 miles, instead of 300."

"And the same amount back," Frank added. "My sitter's already tired."

As daylight broke, we drove through the desert. Eating our breakfast sandwiches as we drove made the miles seem to go by a little faster.

There was more silence and less teasing in the pickup cab than usual. Mom tried to prepare us. "Grandmommy is *very* ill," she said. "Her cancer has gotten worse. Visiting her will not be like when we've seen her ever before."

Mom was right. Grandmommy was not full of life, not enthusiastic, not full of fun. She smiled when we arrived. But she stayed in bed. She looked tired. Sometimes she winced like she had pain. She spoke to each of us, but she wasn't the same. She wasn't vibrant.

We visited awhile, then Dad said, "We'd better go now. We've got a long ride ahead. And you need to rest."

"I'm so-o-o glad you came," Grandmommy said with weak voice. "I'm glad I got to see you all one more time."

"Bye, Grandmommy," we kids chorused as Mom herded us out.

"Bye."

Dad stayed a few more minutes. When he came out, his cheeks were red, his eyes moist. "Thanks for taking care of Mom," he told his aunt.

"I'm glad I can," she said. Her eyes were moist too. "Lately she's been going downhill pretty fast," she added. "We may not have much longer. Since you don't have a phone, would you call me frequently?"

"Yes," Dad said. "I can go to a phone booth."

We weren't very far down the road when Frank asked, "Does Grandmommy really think this is the last time she'll see us?"

"Yes," Dad said. "Her cancer has grown. She's in a lot of pain now, and she doesn't think she will . . ." He choked on the words. Tears slid down his cheek. He pulled out his red handkerchief, wiped his eyes, and blew his nose. He swallowed hard, then spoke again. "She doesn't think she'll live much longer."

We talked about how life just wouldn't seem right without Grandmommy. Dad told us stories about Grandmommy through the years. The memories sparked warmth and laughter and helped the miles go faster—as did eating another batch of sandwiches. We talked about the fun times we'd had with Papa and Grandmommy—Saturday evening get-togethers, picnics, holidays.

We finally drove through Umatilla and approached the Oregon and Washington state line. Suddenly Frank exploded in laughter. Emma frowned at him. "What are you laughing at?"

He tried to talk, but he laughed so hard he couldn't speak. He pointed out the window.

Emma started to read aloud the green sign he pointed toward. "Keep Wash . . ." She burst into laughter too.

Mom and Dad both started to snicker.

Frank finally got words out. "The sign says, 'Keep Washington Green.'" He dissolved into laughter again, then choked out, "Look around. Is there any green thing in any direction?"

I looked left, right, and forward. The sky and river were blue, the rock cliffs gray, and the bunchgrass all a dried tan color.

Emma laughed so hard she was barely able to blurt out, "The only thing green for miles around is the sign."

"Whoever put that sign up is either blind or has a weird sense of humor!" Dad said.

"Or," Mom added, "they put it up when the spring green comes out for a short while."

Every now and again for the rest of the way, one or another started laughing. Or someone blurted, "Keep Washington Green," and we all burst into laughter.

A few days later, we were back in school. Often, over supper, Dad told of his last phone call with his aunt. Sadness seemed to seep out from the boards in the shack.

One afternoon fresh snow piled up. Maybe Mom saw it as a time to lighten the mood. As we finished supper, she asked, "Want some snow ice cream?"

"Yeah!" we answered in near-unison.

She handed Emma and Frank each a large bowl. "Make sure you only get fresh, clean snow. Go out a ways—go beyond where we've been brushing our teeth!"

Emma made a face of disgust. "Oh-h-h, yuk!" she said, half under her breath.

Before long they returned with bowls brimming. "I have more snow than you," Frank taunted.

"No, you don't," Emma countered. "My bowl is bigger than yours."

"No, I got the most!"

"No . . ."

"Enough, you honyocks," Dad interrupted. "You each got snow. Sit down and I'll read you a story while Mom works her magic."

So Dad read. Mom stirred a little milk, sugar, and vanilla flavoring into the snow. And before it had a chance to melt, she served us each a heaping bowl of snow ice cream. I savored each spoonful of sweetness.

A few mornings later the air seemed especially cold. Frost covered the canvas over our bed. I hated to get out from under the covers. Br-r-r-r!

Finally, I jumped out, slid my stockinged feet into boots, and hightailed it into the shack.

"I do believe it's winter," the voice on the radio said. "The mercury reads 17 degrees here at our Pasco studio."

"No wonder it feels so-o-o cold!" Emma exclaimed.

That was bad enough, but, twenty miles north, our thermometer pointed to 7 degrees.

As we all tried to warm up around the oven, Dad grinned. "This summer when you're complaining about it being 98 degrees, I'll remind you about this. Just the thought should cool you off."

Somehow, in the midst of my shivers, I couldn't remember ever being hot.

Unfortunately, 7 degrees with bone-chilling breeze wasn't the worst coldness to blow into our family that winter.

CHAPTER 14

Seeds

D ad faithfully telephoned either his aunt or Papa. The reports on Grandmommy's health became more dire. On February 16 our beloved Grandmommy succumbed to the cancer.

A few days later we made the three-hundred-mile trek to McMinnville to Grandmommy's funeral. If I had attended a funeral before, I didn't remember it. Dad's large family had met often at Papa and Grandmommy's. Each occasion had been full of laughter and joy. This was totally different. Papa was there, but the twinkle in his eyes was gone. The same aunts, uncles, and cousins who had been at earlier family gatherings were there, but the heart of the family joy lay silent. I'd never seen so many tears. I didn't understand everything, but I did grasp that never again would Grandmommy welcome us into her home or into her warm heart.

The trip home gave us time to talk about Grandmommy again. Dad told stories about the art classes she taught, about his washing dishes so she could have more time to fill orders for her oil paintings.

About the meals she cooked. About her love for every member of the family—including the mischievous ones.

"All of our cousins just called her Grandma," I said. "Why do we call her Grandmommy?"

Mom chuckled. "Well, your youngest aunt is just six weeks older than Emma. When Grandmommy realized she and I were going to have babies about the same time, she fussed, 'I can't imagine two little kids running around together and one calling me Mom and the other calling me Grandma. No! I'm not ready to be called Grandma!'

"I don't remember who came up with the idea of calling her Grandmommy," Mom continued, "but she was okay with it. To our family, she's been Grandmommy ever since."

Certainly we would miss Grandmommy! In the three-hundred-mile drive home, tears and laughter mingled as various ones recounted family stories—a mix of sadness at Grandmommy's passing and gratefulness for the years and delights we'd enjoyed. She'd planted a lot of love in our lives. Even at home, remembering Grandmommy and sharing the stories brought warmth in spite of winter cold.

The days went by. At school, more than once my teacher grinned and said, "Helen, now we know you can speak loudly and clearly. Read louder, please."

I'd take a deep breath, picture speaking to the goats and sheep, and read loudly enough that my classmates could hear.

Church every week held extra blessings—besides worshipping, singing, and seeing friends, we could go to the bathroom in comfort and wash our hands in warm, running water.

When winter finally loosened its grasp and spring came, it was welcome! That spring the news talked of more farmers buying land. One family settled on acreage west of Matthews Corner, about three-fourths of a mile southwest of our shack.

That spring a breeze sometimes cooled the air, but rarely did the wind blow hard. A few rain showers dampened the desert . . . and the canvas on our beds. Where the desert was gray-green the previous summer, it boasted the green of new life.

"Things'll be better this year!" Dad said.

I hoped he was right.

"We're here now," he added, "so we can get crops planted earlier this year. We'll also put in rill irrigation—that's corrugations," he told us. "That's the system we used in southern Idaho, and we grew wonderful crops." He smiled, then turned serious again. "And, hopefully, our place in Oregon will sell. Sure would help to have some extra cash!"

"And, hopefully," Mom added, "the wind will stay calm."

Dad contacted a man about leveling the field west of the shack. "I'll be glad to do it," the contractor said, "but with all the new farmers moving in, several others have already contracted with me. You'd have to wait your turn."

Dad agreed to wait. He purchased suction tubes so we'd be ready as soon as the land was prepared. He planted a small field of pinto beans on part of what had been the oat field the year before and started watering the beans with the garden sprinkler.

As we waited, barely a breeze ruffled our hair. Mom planted garden seeds of cool-loving plants—peas, radishes. Later she planted a big garden.

Dad contacted the land leveler occasionally. He was working long days, trying to get to everyone as quickly as he could. We were still on his list, but still waiting. By the time he finally got to our fields, school was out.

We watched as the contractor towed his scraper over the ground, removing all former plants and their roots. When the ground was smooth with a slight slope away from the irrigation ditch, he used a different piece of equipment and dug parallel furrows from the south end of the field to the north.

Dad planted alfalfa by the broadcast method, as he had the oats the previous year. Then he placed one end of small, curved, metal suction pipes in the ditch at the south end of the field. Each pipe suctioned irrigation water out of the ditch into the furrows that Dad called corrugations. The water was supposed to run down the corrugations to the far end of the field. One could tell how far the water got, because the sand was a darker tan where it was wet. To change the water, Dad, Frank, or Emma would move the pipes further across the field to another set of furrows. Water ran slowly down the small corrugations, soaking into the sand. The sand dried quickly and turned back to a lighter color after the water was moved.

The day after the field was planted and watered, the wind came up—the wind which had been nearly absent all spring seemed to be trying to make up for lost time. "Tuck the canvas under your mattress," Dad warned Emma and me. "We don't want your covers to blow across the desert."

A warm breeze dried laundry on the clothesline in a few hours. We brought laundry in off the line and folded it.

The wind strengthened into a gale. Sand pummeled the side of the shack. I pulled Hazel's crib away from the wall and scooted a chair to the window. I stared out—the air was dark with sand. It was obvious where tumbleweeds got their name—a flurry of the round weeds tumbled across the desert. Suddenly a gust screamed and the tumbleweeds raced! Then a strange sight. I blinked and looked again.

"Mom," I yelled. "The washtub's flying!"

Mom glanced out the window. She wheeled around and headed out, slamming the door behind her. An instant later she raced the wind across the desert, her hair standing on end, skirt flying. The wash tub flew and bounced ahead of her. She ran, gaining on the tub, then a gust caught it and it raced further ahead again. She got closer. It took off again. She put on full steam. Finally, she caught hold of a handle as the tub bounced.

She stood there for a long minute, her shoulders heaving. Then she turned and tried to head back to the shack. She leaned into the wind in an effort to move, but the wind blew so hard she couldn't make any headway. Finally, hanging on to the handle for dear life, she pushed the tub down onto the sand and plopped herself into it. There she sat, folded into the metal tub, shoulders still heaving, legs and arms hanging out, hair and apron flying.

The wind kept blowing. Mom sat right there—holding down the washtub, keeping it from flying to some other farm . . . or state.

When the wind finally eased a bit, Mom climbed out of the tub, holding onto the handles with white knuckles. Leaning into the wind, she pushed one leg before the other. Finally she reached the shack. I could hear her at the side of the shack—I guessed she was tying the tub in its place under Emma's and my bed.

"Whew," she said when she slumped through the door. She sat down, breathing heavily. "What a tempest!"

Washtubs weren't the only things the wind blew out of their places. Dad trudged in from the field. He plopped into a chair by the table. Sighed. Closed his eyes. His chin nearly touched his chest.

Mom looked at him questioningly but didn't say a word.

Finally, he looked up at Mom. He sighed again, then spoke in a sad, quavering voice. "So much for that alfalfa seed."

Mom stood there a long moment. "What do you mean?"

"All the seed I planted yesterday is gone. Blown away. All of it."

CHAPTER 15

Bad News, Good News

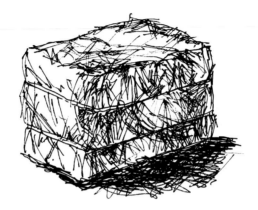

Dad's shoulders slumped as he gave Mom the news that all the seed he'd planted the day before had blown away in the strong wind.

"Surely some is still there," Mom encouraged.

"Nope," Dad said. "It's probably all about halfway to Canada." He paused. "All that seed wasted. I'll have to replant."

After a couple minutes of silence, Mom asked, "And what about the beans?"

"The sand cut off a lot of the little plants, but there still are some. We'll water them as much as we can. Maybe we can save at least part of that crop."

"We can be thankful for that," Mom said.

Dad just sat there, head down.

On a calm day nearly a week later, Dad broadcast alfalfa seed across the field again. He, Emma, and Frank changed the water frequently, trying to get the alfalfa to grow before another windstorm hit. But that presented another problem—the water soaked down in the sand so fast that it took a long time for the water to get to the end of the corrugations. And even if the water eventually got to the end, the plants there didn't get as much moisture as the plants closer to the source.

Summer moved on day by day, windstorm by windstorm. The wind was worse, way worse, than the summer before. Our family wasn't the only one having wind struggles, but just because the neighbors were having trouble raising the money to buy more seed didn't make our financial strain any easier. The fourth planting of alfalfa grew fairly well near the south end of the field where it got the most water. But it was so late there'd hardly be any crop that year. The north end blew out again.

Besides planting and replanting alfalfa, other things needed to be done also. Frank sheared the sheep. One or another fed, watered, and milked the animals. The garden grew . . . and so did the weeds—we all got in on weeding. Mom got out needle and thread, and she and Emma mended rips in clothing wearing thin.

"I wish we'd brought the sewing machine when we moved," Emma said. "Mending would go a lot faster."

Mom grinned. "And where would you put the treadle machine?"

Emma looked around the single room and sighed.

"This won't last forever," Mom encouraged. She smiled and her eyes took on a sparkle. "Someday we'll have a real house again. And our beds will be inside and out of the weather. Someday we'll have the sewing machine, the couch, the piano." Her needle went down through thin fabric . . . up . . . down . . . up . . . down. She looked up again. "But we already have something pretty wonderful!" she exclaimed.

Emma looked up. Her eyes narrowed. One corner of her mouth raised, the other lowered in a grimace. "What's wonderful?"

"We're all together as a family!" Mom said. "And we're all healthy. Someday we'll say, 'We overcame . . . together!'"

In silence, Mom's and Emma's needles kept at their work. "But when?" Emma finally asked.

Mom's hands stilled. She looked up. "I don't know when," she said. "But we'll work to make it as soon as possible."

Laundry was easier in summer than in winter . . . as long as the clothes dried and we got them in before another dust storm hit. By late afternoons, we were eager to cool off in the canal . . . also known as bathing.

Early summer, the apricots came on at Ringold. We went and they hired us to pick again. The more fruit we picked, the more we got paid. We worked hard and by the end of a day went home with some cash and some fruit. Again, Mom and I canned fruit and Dad, Emma, and Frank went back to pick and buy more. The orchard manager had said we could eat all the fruit we wanted while we picked. We all enjoyed copious amounts of the sweetness of tree-ripened apricots. Frank ate so many that he moaned and groaned all the way home.

One afternoon after apricot harvest was complete a pickup drove up to our place. A tall, muscular man crawled out. Dad went to greet him. Frank followed close behind.

"Hi. I'm Jack Taylor. I was just stopping by to see if you had any hay you need to have stacked."

"No," Dad said. "We planted some hay . . . and replanted, but we don't have anything near big enough to make bales out of yet."

"Sounds like you're in the same boat as a lot of us," Jack said. "A lot of land leveling went on this spring. The little bit of ground cover this desert had before was disturbed. Then all this wind! Have you heard the reports? It's the windiest summer on record—winds up to seventy miles per hour!"

"Yeah, I've heard . . . and I've felt the wind."

"Some of the farmers have planted three or four times," Jack said, "and blown out every time."

Dad sighed. "We're one of them—we've pretty much spent everything on seed . . . and it's all blown off to the east. Don't know how we're going to survive the winter."

Jack nodded. "Same spot as a lot of us here in the Columbia Basin," he said. "Families are doing all kinds of things to make a go of farming. Some husbands have gotten full-time jobs and their wives are doing most of the farming. The husbands help as much as they can. And a lot of women who've always been housewives are looking for jobs in town to keep their families from starving."

"It sure is a different way of life," Dad said. He sighed. Then his eyes brightened, "Speaking of work, do *you* need some help?"

"What do you have in mind?"

"My boy here," he motioned toward Frank. "He's a good worker. And we sure could use the money."

Jack looked Frank up one side and down the other. "Naw. He's too small. The bales probably weigh more than he does."

Jack, come to find out, was one of the new neighbors this year. He had a truck and was stacking hay to supplement his family's income. He was trying to make a go of farming in the desert just like everyone else.

Farmers seemed to be the only occupants in our area who struggled financially. Construction was one of the industries that was booming. In June, radio broadcasters talked about the new hump yard nearing completion. It was the first modern electronic freight classification hump yard in the Pacific Northwest. On June 21, 1955, the Burlington Northern Santa Fe Railway hump yard was dedicated.

Also during that summer, three major fertilizer and petroleum tank farms had sprouted up. Not only had their construction provided employment, they would require ongoing workers.

The month after the hump yard was dedicated, radio newscasters noted more transportation progress—the Umatilla Bridge across the Columbia River was dedicated on July 15, 1955. It joined Oregon and Washington, and the governors of both states took part in the dedication.

"Progress," Dad said, "is often both good and bad."

"Why do you say that?" Emma asked.

"Well," Dad explained, "the new bridge eases life for people who live across the river from each other near Umatilla on the Oregon side of the river, and Plymouth or Paterson on the, Washington side. It also shortens the distance between Pasco and Umatilla, which means it'll also be closer from here to Portland. So some shipping by truck will probably be less expensive."

"What's bad about that?" Frank asked.

"Nothing's bad about that part," Dad said, "but, it's also a toll bridge. So, every time someone drives over it, they'll have to stop and pay a fee. Also, by the bridge being open for traffic, it puts two ferries out of business. So two families lost their income."

As summer moved on, in the afternoon, Hazel and I often walked to the mailbox at the end of our quarter-mile driveway. If she wanted to go with me to get the mail, she had to agree to hold my hand when we got near the canal. Some days there was nothing but air in the mailbox. When I told Mom, "Nothing but air mail," she smiled and said, "No mail is better than bills!"

Occasionally we received newsy letters from Aunt Thelma, Mom's sister. She filled us in on the aunt, uncle, and cousin happenings on Mom's side of the family. Sometimes I recognized Grandma Miller's "squarish" handwriting on an envelope. Mom would sit down right away and read aloud to Hazel and me about Grandma's latest adventures, then we'd hear the letter over again at supper.

One day we got a letter addressed in handwriting I didn't recognize. Mom slid her finger under the seal, opened the envelope, and pulled out a handwritten letter. She started to read it aloud, then gasped mid-sentence. She read on silently. Tears came to her eyes. She stared at the letter like she couldn't believe what she read. Her eyes moved to the top again, then down the page.

Finally, Mom laid the letter on the kitchen counter and explained. "Your cousin, Carolyn, went to the hospital to have her tonsils taken out. Unfortunately, she started bleeding and they couldn't stop the bleeding. She died." Mom wiped her eyes. "She was only ten."

Mom told me more about my uncle, aunt, and cousin. I didn't know Carolyn well, but she was only a year and a half older than I. It felt unbelievable that someone that age could die.

The funeral had already happened by the time we got the letter. All Mom could do to comfort her brother and his wife was to write letters to them.

Finally, a few days later, some good news. "Someday whoever lives here is going to need a shop on this place," Dad said. "Your Uncle Max is going to build a shop, and we can live in it through this next winter."

"Has to be better than sleeping outside!" Frank said.

"It was so-o-o cold last winter!" Emma added. She shivered at the thought. "Can we move in before cold weather hits?"

"Should be able to," Dad responded.

A few days later, Uncle Max arrived. He and Dad discussed building plans, ordered supplies, and set to work. Max added humor to our life. Mom cooked enough for him too. He slept under a canopy on his pickup.

The shop's concrete floor was a simple rectangle, a little wider than the shack was long. It was about twice as long as it was wide. After the floor cured, Max and Dad laid boards on the concrete. They built the framework for one wall, then slowly raised it up and fastened it in place. Then another wall.

Frank repeatedly helped for a while, went to change the water in the field, then returned to help with building again.

The action gave Hazel and me something to watch over and over again, day after day.

On the east side nearest the road, Max framed around two large areas.

"What are you doing?" Frank asked.

"Making a spot for garage doors," Max answered. "We'll cover them up for now, but when we get ready to turn this into a shop, we'll cut out the walls here and put in garage doors."

One morning when they were working on the roof, Jack Taylor drove up again. Dad and Max waved. Mr. Taylor crawled out of his truck, walked over to the shop, and looked up at the roof. "My hired man didn't show up this morning. Is it okay with you if I try out your son for the day?"

"That'd be fine," Dad said.

Mr. Taylor looked at Frank. "Are you willing to give bucking bales a try?" Then he added, "Just for today."

"Sure," Frank said.

"Can you grab something for a lunch quickly?"

"Yes, sir," Frank answered. He scrambled down the ladder. "I'll be right back." He raced toward the shack. In nothing flat he was back, brown bag in hand. "I'm ready."

That evening Frank looked bushed.

"So, how'd it go?" Mom asked.

"I'm hot and tired!" he said. "Those bales are heavy! They weigh about a hundred pounds." He grabbed his washcloth and the soap and headed for the canal.

At supper Frank ate like he hadn't eaten in a week.

"When was the last time you fed this kid?" Uncle Max asked with an impish grin.

"Not so long ago," Mom said.

Max chuckled.

With food, Frank's energy seemed to revive some. "Mr. Taylor is strong!" he said. "He throws those bales around like they're toothpicks. And, by the way, he says I can go to work tomorrow too!"

"You must have done him a good job!" Dad said.

"I sure tried. It was hard work. By the end of the day, I learned how to use my body weight to help move the bales, not just lift with my arms."

"Do you realize what you did today?" Mom asked.

"Yeah—bucked bales."

"But more than that," Mom said. "By working hard, paying attention, and learning, you created an opportunity for yourself. That's the stuff success is made of."

Emma did all the milking that evening, and Dad fed and watered the animals. Frank went to bed early.

Frank must have worked hard! I thought. *He must be* really *tired! He didn't tease anyone all evening!*

CHAPTER 16

The Move

Soon the shop had a roof. Then windows and front and back doors.

Inside, the north two-thirds was one big room. The plan was for it to become a shop someday. For now, we would sleep there.

The south third would have electric wall heaters. It would be our kitchen and living room. The kitchen corner held cabinets—even a sink under a window in the west wall. Though there wouldn't be running water at first, the sink and faucets gave hope.

"Hm-m-m," Uncle Max said as I looked around the shop-house one afternoon. "Maybe I'll move in here and let you guys stay in your shack."

I glared at him.

"Besides, you're used to sleeping outside. Maybe you wouldn't like sleeping indoors."

I ran back to the shack and choked out, "Mom, is Uncle Max going to move into the shop? Are we going to keep sleeping outside?"

Mom grinned. "Did Max tell you that?"

"Yeah."

"Was he grinning when he said it?"

"Yeah."

"You do know he's a big tease, don't you?"

"Yeah."

Mom grinned again. "Sometimes I think your brother spent too much time with him."

"So, he was just teasing me?"

"I'd guess so," Mom said. She chuckled. "Remember what Grandmommy used to say about Max?"

"No."

"She used to say, 'Max could tease a fencepost until it cried.'"

And so it continued. Uncle Max teased anyone . . . anytime. The impish grin and the sparkle in his eyes usually gave him away. A deep, happy chuckle would follow.

But sometimes he was at least somewhat serious. When he and Dad finished the main part of the shop-house, Max asked Mom, "Are you ready to move into your castle?"

"Doesn't exactly look like a castle to me." Mom grinned. "But, considering where we've been, it's a great upgrade. And, yes, I'm ready to move in!"

"Could you and the girls help clean up tomorrow?"

"Certainly."

"We'll get the heavy stuff out, but if you'll sweep up the smaller stuff, it sure would help."

With sparkle in her eyes and delight in her voice, Mom answered, "We'll be glad to!"

The next morning, when Dad came in for breakfast, he'd already changed the irrigation in the field. "Finally," he said, "though the crop is sparse, looks like some of the alfalfa is growing pretty well. If it can survive the storms, we'll at least have a little crop."

After breakfast, Hazel and I picked up little pieces of lumber and whatever else lay around. Mom and Emma brushed and dusted off windowsills, swept and mopped the concrete floor, washed the windows. The place even smelled clean.

That afternoon Max and Dad moved the kitchen range, refrigerator, table, and chairs into the new kitchen. Hazel and I stood on the sidelines watching, until the big things were moved. Then we carried the washbasin, dishpan, and other small things.

When Frank got home from bucking bales, the shack was nearly empty. "Wow," Frank declared, "a guy leaves for a few hours and his family moves."

"Yeah," Emma answered, "and you didn't help a bit!"

"And," he responded with smug confidence, "I'm not going to help tomorrow either. Mr. Taylor said I'm doing a good job and I can keep working for him!"

"Your paycheck will help pay bills," Dad said. "I'm glad you're working hard for him!"

The next morning we tore beds apart. "Good riddance to the canvas!" Emma said.

"Yeah!" I added. "It felt really heavy."

"Yes," Emma said. "I'm glad we had it, but I'm really glad we're done with it!"

The sun shone. A light breeze cooled us some. We hung wool blankets on the clothesline to air. We washed sheets and washable quilts and hung them to dry. Then we wiped down bed frames and springs with damp cloths to get rid of the dust and dirt before hauling them into our "shop house."

I'd gotten so used to lying on my side at night and looking up at the stars, that I sort of missed seeing them. But I knew I wouldn't miss the view when winter came!

A few days later, Dad strung wire near the ceiling, and Mom and Emma hung curtains and blankets on it. We had "bedrooms" again. We could get dressed without anyone having to go outside or turn around and close their eyes.

On the outside of our "castle," work continued. Max and Dad wrapped the walls with black tarpaper, nailing light-colored wood lath boards every fifteen inches or so from top to bottom. The building looked striped like a zebra—only the stripes were straight up and down.

At the end of their work days, Dad and Max began storing their tools in the shack. Mom put garden tools and wash tubs there also. "This winter when it's bitter cold, we can put the washing machine in the shack!" she exulted.

One day the mail carrier drove to our house rather than leaving letters in the box at the road.

"Mom," I called, "the mailman's bringing a *big* package." He carried a big box about three feet square to the house.

Mom met him at the door.

"Your mail wouldn't fit in your box today," he said. He smiled, handing the huge box to Mom.

When Mom took the box, it lurched upward, like she was expecting it to be heavy, but it wasn't.

"And here's a couple letters, too," he added.

"Thank you," Mom said. She set the box on a chair and looked at the address label. She started to say something, but no words came out. She just stood there, staring. Tears dropped onto the box.

CHAPTER 17

For Me?

M om wiped her tears.

"What is it?" I asked.

Mom took a deep breath. She cleared her throat. "Helen, I think you'll have some different dresses for school this year," she said. "Would you please get the scissors?"

She cut the string and opened the box flaps.

I stood on tiptoe and saw soft pink fabric with a lace-edged collar.

Mom picked it up gently, like it was something precious. She held up the dress and motioned me close. She held the dress up to my shoulders. "It might be just a tad big, but you'll grow into it," she said.

"It's for me?"

"Yes." She picked up dress after dress and held them up—a blue dress, a red dress, a plaid dress, and on and on. They were all about my size. Then there were pedal pushers, blouses, underwear, socks, shoes.

Shocked by the array of lovely clothes, I asked, "Are they *all* my size?"

"We'll have you try them on after you clean up this afternoon," Mom said.

"Where'd they come from?"

"They all belonged to your cousin," Mom said. "After Carolyn died, her mother wrote and asked if you might be able to use her clothes."

Some of the items were a little big for me. Some fit perfectly. After wearing the same dress to church every week, I felt excited that I had different dresses to wear. In fact, I could wear a new dress every week for a couple months. I'd never had so many clothes and I'd never had such nice clothes.

In the field, the alfalfa still struggled. The south end of the field showed a lot of green. At the north end where the water supply was less dependable, the field was mostly the tan of sand. The plants in the bean field were sparse also.

The garden didn't do much better. Mom replanted some things when the seeds blew away, but even the things which had grown were ripped and stunted by the wind and blowing sand.

With all six of us in the same building at night, I sometimes heard Mom and Dad whispering to each other. Things like, "We got an electric bill today. How are we going to pay it?"

"The peaches up at Ringold Farms should be about ripe. I'll check to see if they need pickers again."

A couple evenings later at supper, Dad asked, "Remember how good the peaches tasted last year?"

Thinking about the flavor clinched the deal. When Frank headed out to buck bales, the rest of us headed to the orchard. Not only would we earn some money to help pay bills, we could buy peaches to can and to eat.

The wind didn't care whether or not there were workers on ladders. At the orchard, we donned picking buckets with straps over our shoulders. The buckets were about as big as I was. When I climbed a ladder and the wind blew hard, I held onto a limb with one hand and picked fuzzy, golden fruit with the other. Others would fill their buckets before clambering down. They walked to a bin, unbuckled the canvas bottom of the bucket, and emptied the contents gently so as not to bruise the ripe fruit. I was small enough that the picking bucket got too heavy to carry if I filled it more than half full.

Sometimes Mom, from her ladder perch, kept an eye on Hazel's ramblings in the tall grass under the trees. She'd talk to her and keep her nearby most of the time. Now and then I'd hear her call to Emma, Dad, or me, "Do you see Hazel?"

One of us could generally answer, "Yes, she's right here by my ladder."

To keep Hazel occupied and safe, sometimes Mom asked me to quit picking peaches for a while and play with her.

At noon, we sat on the grass in the shade of a peach tree and ate our sandwiches. Since the boss had said we could eat all the peaches we wanted, for dessert we ate sweet, juicy, flavorful, tree-ripened peaches. I stood up and leaned over as I slurped the soft fruit, savoring its flavor. In spite of the stickiness on my chin and shirt, I smiled at the sweet deliciousness. Fortunately, there was a water faucet nearby. Running water—that was a treat in itself!

Afternoons were hot. The shade of the trees and the breeze off the nearby Columbia River helped us handle the heat. The rewards kept us working.

Nearly every afternoon—except for Thursdays, when we cleaned the church—we drove home with more peaches. We washed up and started filling quart jars and heating water for canning. For supper dessert we enjoyed a bowl of sweet, juicy peaches. Some liked them best with milk poured on top. I liked them best of all just plain and juicy and sweet. M-m-m-m-mmm. And at home with the sliced peaches in a bowl, they didn't drip down my chin and make me sticky all over.

We kept canning peaches until time for worship. After worship Mom said, "You all go on to bed. I'll finish up here."

I scurried off to bed. Sometimes Mom looked really tired the next morning. I don't know how long into the night she worked, but in the morning there'd be more jars of golden peaches than there had been the night before.

When the last peach was picked off the trees, I still liked peaches!

One August afternoon when Hazel and I went after the mail, I noted the "squarish" handwriting on one of the letters. In the house, I announced, "We got a letter from Grandma Miller!" Mom wiped her hands on her apron, sat down, and read the letter aloud.

Earlier in the summer Grandma's letters told of her visits with our aunts, uncles, and cousins. By mid-August, she wrote about preparations for teaching in the new school year.

Hm-m-m. It was about time for our school to start too. I liked learning. I just wished I could go to school without ever having to say anything to anyone.

One evening Dad announced at supper, "We made some new plans today."

We kids, curious, gave him our attention.

"Now that the Olsons have moved away, it was going to be just us driving the twenty miles to school twice a day. But Mom and I met a farm wife today who got a job in town to help make ends meet. Their farm is north of us, and she drives into town to her job every day. She drives right by our place, and her work is only half a mile or so from your school. She works later than school hours, but we offered to pay her some if you honyocks could ride with her in the mornings. That sounded good to her, and it will save us a trip a day. So, when school starts, you'll need to be out by the mailbox promptly at 7:45 waiting for Mrs. Morse."[2]

Even though most mothers in the nation stayed home and took care of their kids, husbands, and houses, the rigors of trying to transform desert into farms had chased many happy homemakers into looking for jobs in town.

---

2 Not her real name.

A few days after Dad told us about Mrs. Morse, I rode into town with Mom. In a grocery store aisle, I spotted the homeliest woman my third-grade eyes had ever seen. She looked angry.

I suddenly had a desire to walk close beside Mom. But when Mom looked up, she saw the woman, smiled, and said in a friendly tone, "Good afternoon, Mrs. Morse."

Mrs. Morse? My heart suddenly felt like it was beating fast . . . up in my throat. *Is this the Mrs. Morse we'll be riding to school with?* I wondered.

"Good afternoon." She smiled. Still, to me, she looked mean.

"We told our children they'd be riding to school in the mornings with you," Mom said.

They visited briefly. "So, Tuesday morning the kids will be waiting for you. At 7:45, right?

"That's great," Mrs. Morse replied. "Looking forward to having some company."

Suddenly, my chest felt tight. Just seeing this woman in the store scared me. Was she a mean person? How could we handle riding to school with her every day? Dread filled me every time I thought about riding to school with Mrs. Morse.

CHAPTER 18

Brr-rr-rr

J ack Taylor continued to hire Frank to buck bales until school started. "Thanks for your hard work," Jack said when he dropped Frank off the last day. "You're a good worker. I'd be happy to keep you on, but better you get an education!"

Each time Frank got paid, Dad asked for his check. Frank handed it over, and Dad gave it to Mom. She made every penny stretch as far as possible. Frank's wages helped buy groceries and pay bills.

The first day of school, we waited at the side of the road a few minutes before 7:45. Moments later a car drove up. Frank opened the back door closest to us and slid across the seat. I crawled in behind him and scooted to the middle where I'd, hopefully, be safe between Frank and Emma.

"Good morning!" Mrs. Morse exclaimed. "How are you this morning?"

Frank and Emma responded. Silent, I kept my eyes on Mrs. Morse. Would she be as mean as she looked to me?

"Now, let me see if I remember your names. She glanced in the mirror making eye contact with my sister. "You're Emma, right?"

"Yes."

"What year are you in school?"

"I'm a sophomore."

"What are you looking forward to this school year?"

The conversation continued, then Mrs. Morse questioned, "And you, young man. You must be Frank?"

"That's right."

"And what do you enjoy most about school?"

"Recess. Especially when we play ball."

Mrs. Morse laughed. "What position do you like best?"

"I like pitching!"

"Pitching? Can you strike out the batters?"

"I could sometimes last year. But I've been practicing this summer. I think I'll do better this year."

"Practicing, huh? Good for you. Practice makes perfect, you know."

Frank laughed. "Yeah, Mom and Dad say that too. I don't have a softball, but chunks of the pavement are breaking off the edges of our airstrip. So I pick up a piece of pavement about the size of a ball and throw it at a place I marked on the ditch bank."

The conversation went on for several miles. I hoped they'd keep talking until we arrived. No such luck.

"Well, there's one more of you. Young lady in the middle, wasn't your name Helen?"

I nodded.

"She can't hear your head rattle," Frank said.

"Uh-huh," I whispered.

"What grade are you in?"

I swallowed hard.

"She's in third grade," Emma answered for me.

Every morning, Mrs. Morse greeted us with a smile. She talked with us like we were intelligent human beings. Her eyes sparkled as Emma and Frank conversed with her. She asked me a question every now and again, too. By the end of the week, I spoke brief answers loud enough so she could hear me if I leaned forward.

On occasion Mom had said, "Don't judge a book by its cover." I'd never understood what she meant. Mrs. Morse explained it to me without even knowing it. Within a few days I didn't notice what Mrs. Morse looked like. She respected people of all ages—even bashful kids who were too shy to speak loud enough for her to hear. Her heart was kind—she was beautiful.

I began to look forward to the ride to school. I returned her smile. Sometimes I even said "Good morning" before she did!

In mid-September, just a couple weeks after our school started, Columbia Basin College opened in Pasco. It was housed in buildings formerly occupied by the Pasco Naval Air Station that had been decommissioned after World War II. As the tenth community college in the state of Washington, Pasco leaders hoped it would be a help to local students and a boon to the economy. It would be a few years before any of us would have any possibility of helping with that boon.

Polio outbreaks happened from time to time in different places throughout the United States and the world. We were fortunate to not know anyone who had contracted the disease. But, occasionally, I heard newscasters talk about another outbreak. Trials of Jonas Salk's polio vaccine proved to nearly eradicate the disease in those who had been vaccinated. In 1955, the vaccine became available all over the country. Emma, Frank, and I received the vaccine at school, along with every other student who had a permission slip from their parents. For us, the tiny injection in the upper arm was more nuisance than painful.

In the afternoons after our school finished for the day, Dad or Mom picked us up. On the way home one afternoon, Dad said, "We have a new job for this weekend. The pinto beans in our field are so sparse we can't afford to have a combine come in and harvest them. Remember how we gleaned beans last year?"

"Yeah," we all responded.

"Well, now you're experienced help." He grinned impishly. "We get to do it again. Only this time, we get to harvest our whole field."

We each wandered down a row of beans, placing bean pods from the infrequent dried plants in gunnysacks. When we finished in the field for the day, Frank or Emma lifted the burlap bags above their shoulders and thrust them down against the pavement. That helped separate some of the beans from the hulls and stems. But the rest we accomplished in the same manner as the year before—dumping the beans onto the pavement and stomping our feet in our food.

When we completed the job each evening, we gathered the beans into clean bags and stored them in the house, then stashed the chaff that hadn't blown away with the other animal food underneath a protective canvas.

We also managed a fair bit of complaining. When we came in one evening, Mom was figuring at the table. She picked up the bills and checkbook and lay them on a corner of the counter. She had a far-off look in her eyes as she stirred a pot of soup. We kids continued griping. "You know," Mom said in a quiet but attention-grabbing tone, "come winter, you may be very glad we have beans."

Something about the tone of her voice made me wonder what winter might bring.

Potato harvest was in full swing for those farmers who got their fields planted before the wind hit. Dad got a temporary job in a potato warehouse. The company he worked for had a storage facility for carrots as well. Not only did Dad come home with paychecks, his employer also gave the employees cull potatoes and carrots. We stored the gunnysacks full of potatoes and carrots in the bedroom area of the shop-house since it had no heat.

Mornings often felt chilly as we crawled out of bed, but it was so much better than sleeping outside that nobody complained. We simply jumped out of bed and hurried to the electric heater in the kitchen. Unfortunately, the jaunts to the outhouse were farther than they had been from the shack.

Sometimes it felt chilly as we walked to the road and waited for Mrs. Morse, but coat, hat, and mittens kept us reasonably comfortable. Then November started out mild—on the ninth, the high temperature hit 68 degrees. Four days later the high temp was 9. The low plummeted to 10 degrees *below* zero. For a week, the temperature never got *up* to 32 degrees—the freezing point.

Even inside the shop, when I woke in the mornings, I could see my own breath. I always hoped someone else had made it to the outhouse just before me and melted the frost off the seat.

Along with the cold came snow—tiny flakes of dry snow that didn't pile up very fast.

The cold complicated every task, including brushing teeth. Whatever the weather, I wasn't fond of traipsing outside with toothbrush and plastic cup of water and spitting in the sand. When the temperature was below zero, I brushed and shivered. When snow blew horizontally, I shivered worse and brushed faster. If there'd been a speed toothbrushing sport in the Olympics, I would have been a contender for gold!

All the coats and mittens we owned could not make us comfortable outside. "Br-r-r, it's cold!" I complained.

"Yes, it is," Frank responded. "But aren't you thankful we aren't sleeping outside this winter?"

"Yes!!!"

"At least we don't get wet!" Emma added. "We have walls around us and a roof over our heads!"

The thought of sleeping outside in this weather made me shiver more. "And no wind inside!" I added.

Just thinking about the previous winter helped me put our blessings in perspective. That reminded me of the blue flower and my observation that there's beauty everywhere—some places you just have to look a lot harder. *Walls and roof are part of the beauty here and now,* I concluded.

A moment later, Frank looked at me. "And you can be thankful you get to stay inside and help Mom," he said, "and don't have to go milk the goats and help with the outside chores when it's zero and snowing and blowing."

I shivered. Setting the table and helping wash dishes had never before seemed so glamorous!

CHAPTER 19

Merry Christmas

One morning Mom drained the last of the cod liver oil into a spoon. She held it toward me. I knew from experience that grumbling or trying to get out of swallowing the nasty tasting liquid would get me nowhere. I opened my mouth like a baby bird waiting for a worm—but with much less enthusiasm. As usual, I gulped down the cod liver oil, grabbed my glass of milk, and chugged down several swallows, trying to get rid of the putrid taste.

Mom glanced at Dad. "That's the last of the cod liver oil," she said.

He looked thoughtful. "Maybe we'll just have to get along without it for a while."

I thought I saw happy gleams in Frank's and Emma's eyes. We all just sat there innocently—quiet was the only way to stay innocent. And I surely didn't want to take a chance on Mom or Dad figuring out how they could afford another bottle of cod liver oil. There were advantages to running low on money!

Food selection was *not* one of the advantages. For breakfast, we had oatmeal mush with goat milk. Some of us weren't very fond of goat milk, but it's what we had. There wasn't any point in complaining—we didn't have money to buy cow's milk. But we enjoyed our home-canned peaches and apricots.

For other meals, we had pinto beans, potatoes, and carrots. When we got tired of beans, potatoes, and carrots, we could choose carrots, potatoes, and beans. Or carrots, beans, and potatoes. Fortunately, Mom was a good cook, but there's a limit to how many ways you can serve those three ingredients if you don't have much else to add to them.

Mom had used up the wheat and the white flour with which she had previously baked. Somewhere, she had gotten some rye. She ground the rye into flour and made rye bread. But the bread made with only rye flour was very dark and very heavy.

"Why have you been eating by yourself lately?" Emma asked Frank one afternoon on the way home from school.

"'Cause I don't want the others to see my food—that dark, heavy bread. And the sandwich filling—forever beans, beans, beans . . . day after day, mashed beans in my sandwich."

At the dinner table during Thanksgiving break, someone asked, "What are we going to do for Christmas this year?"

Mom and Dad glanced at each other. Dad cleared his throat. "Money's awfully tight this year."

"But we can still have Christmas," Mom added. "This year, let's cut pictures out of the Sears and Roebuck catalogue of what we'd *like* to give each other. Or draw pictures."

"You mean, no gifts at all?" Frank asked.

"Just think . . ." Mom smiled. "Gifts are fun to give and fun to get. But half the fun of giving is figuring out what someone would really like and choosing something that would be special to them. We'll still get to have all that fun."

Mom's optimism was contagious. "We can give fancy things we can't afford to buy," I said.

"Yes," Mom said. "And, by the way, I've saved envelopes our mail has come in. We can put the pictures in envelopes and decorate the envelopes with our own art."

"Can we have a tree this year?" Emma asked. "We have room for one now."

"Hm-m-m. I don't know about that," Mom said. "But I'll see if just before Christmas they're cheap enough that we can get one."

The Sears catalogue got to be a popular item. As the days went by, more and more pages were torn out of it. The stack of envelopes Mom set out diminished.

I felt both excited and puzzled when I looked at the catalogue. And sometimes just dreamed of what I'd like to give. I could choose tools for Dad. Or a book—he loved to read. A really nice dress for Mom—she had to mend hers a lot lately. Or a pretty bottle of pricey perfume. Maybe bicycles for Emma and Frank. Or what about a model airplane for Frank? Or a softball and mitt? How about a dress for Emma? Or perfume? Or a jigsaw puzzle? Maybe a ball for Hazel. Or a tricycle—she'd be big enough to use one before long. I turned the catalog pages, then started over. Coats! In case any more horrible cold was coming, everyone ought to get a really warm coat and hat and a pair of mittens. And boots that were taller than any of the snow banks had been so far. Choices, choices.

Just before Christmas break, as we drove home from school one afternoon, my stomach growled.

"Can't wait for beans, potatoes, and carrots, huh?" Frank teased.

I jabbed him in the ribs.

At least we're not going hungry, I reminded myself. *And, even if we have nothing else for Christmas, we'll at least be able to eat . . . even if dinner is beans, potatoes, and carrots.*

Dad turned the pickup into our driveway, crossed the irrigation canal, bore right, turned to the left, and approached the shop house. "What's that big box on the porch?" Frank asked.

Dad glanced toward the porch. "I don't know."

"It's nothing we left there," Mom added.

We kids jumped out of the pickup and headed toward the porch, bent over the huge box, and pulled open the flaps.

We gasped. We stared into the box . . . dumb with shock.

It was filled with food.

Finally, we bent over the box and started exploring the contents. There was fresh fruit and vegetables—oranges, apples, cranberries, yams, celery, onions, lettuce, tomatoes. There was a ham, a bunch of canned vegetables, flour, sugar, shortening, popcorn, hot chocolate mix, and a bag of Christmas candies.

We couldn't believe our eyes. I jabbed Frank in the ribs again. "Think we're having beans, potatoes, and carrots for supper?"

He grinned with delight. "Don't think so!"

"Who would have brought it?" Mom asked.

We looked for a card. It only said, "Have a Merry Christmas." We had no idea who gifted us with kindness. It could have been anyone. It was common knowledge in the area that the wind had ruined crops and that many of the farmers were struggling just to eat. Someone knew. Someone cared. And they reached out to help.

We had crisp, fresh salad with our potato soup that night. And we each got to choose a piece of candy.

Christmas Eve afternoon, Mom and we kids piled into the pickup. Mom drove to a Christmas tree lot. "You kids stay here," she said.

The tree salesman, bundled to the hilt against a frigid breeze, sat on the running board, hunched against his truck. He stood as Mom approached. They spoke to each other. "Sh-h-h." Frank whispered. "Don't say a word." He cranked the window open a hair. Just then the salesman said, "It's Christmas Eve. There's not much left here, but if you'll take a tree, it will help me clean up."

"How much?" Mom asked.

"Not a dime," he said. He motioned to the few scraggly trees left. "You'll help me clean up if you just take one."

"Are you sure? I'll pay if I can afford it."

"I'm positive."

She chose a tree. "Thank you, sir!"

"You're welcome. Thanks for helping me clear out my lot."

Sure looked to me like he had twinkles in his eyes.

At home, we stood the tree in a bucket, scrounged chunks of pavement to put around it so it would stand up, and poured water into the container. We turned the scraggliest side toward the wall. Mom popped popcorn from the Christmas box. We strung it and a few cranberries and wrapped them around the tree. We cut construction paper strips, made multicolored chains, and wrapped them around the tree too. Then festively decorated envelopes began appearing on various branches.

Christmas—a magical time. We had a Christmas tree. We had walls around us and a roof over our heads so we didn't feel the wind or the rain . . . even at night. We had room to wiggle without tripping over someone else's feet and room to play Crokinole and other games.

On Christmas eve we opened envelopes filled with pictures of all kinds of delights. Together, we talked, laughed, and shared our hopes and dreams more than any other Christmas I remembered.

On Christmas day, for dinner we enjoyed variety, including Mom's homemade apple pie. The wish of the donors of the box was granted—we had a very Merry Christmas.

1956

CHAPTER 20

Back to the Shack?

We ate the fragile fresh produce within days. Not a leaf of lettuce was wasted. Apples and oranges lasted longer. Mom rationed the staple contents of the box so we had variety for months. And candy, one piece at a time, for weeks.

Winter was colder than the year before. When the mercury in the thermometer plummeted to *minus* 10 degrees, we thanked God that it hadn't been that cold the winter before when we slept outside. But when the temperature dropped that low, the electric bills shot higher. There was no fruit to pick, no bales to buck, no work in a potato shed.

"You may notice something different in the outhouse," Mom mentioned one morning. "We've run out of toilet paper. So the old Sears catalog is in the toilet paper can."

Frank snickered. "At least we'll have something to look at."

Emma grimaced. "But who wants to look at anything when it's ten below zero and you're just trying to get your job done!"

Spring eventually started winning the temperature battles with winter. Those who did the animal chores donned fewer layers.

They had to break the ice on the animals' water less frequently. Just when it seemed things were looking up, Dad dropped another bombshell.

"Things have changed," he said. "Max needs to farm his own land now. So we need to move to our own farm."

"*Our* farm?" Frank's eyebrows scrunched closer together. He frowned.

"Yep," Dad said. "We need to get our own farm."

"But you're still not a veteran."

"You're right," Dad said, "but the Bureau of Reclamation supervises this farmland, and now they're letting people who aren't veterans buy a farm . . . after it's been turned down three times by veterans."

Frank frowned. "So, we get the reject land?"

Mom smirked.

Dad snickered. "I suppose you could say that. Anyway, we've applied to get our own farm."

"Will it have a house on it?" Emma asked.

"No, it'll be raw land, like when we first moved here."

"Meaning . . ." Frank's voice was full of question. ". . . we break sod all over again?"

"Yep."

"And we fight the wind all over again?"

"Yep."

"And the sand?"

"Yep."

Dad let that thought simmer in our minds for a minute before he went on. "But there's one difference from when we first started here—I've learned we need to do some things differently."

"Like what?" Frank asked.

"For one, we'll not irrigate with corrugations. They can work where there's heavy soil, but they don't work very well here in the sand. We'll water with sprinklers."

"Where will we live?" Emma asked.

"We'll move the shack."

I sighed. *The shack again? Will we sleep outside again?*

Emma looked perplexed. "So . . . if we can't afford toilet paper, how are we going to buy a farm?"

"That's the good news," Dad said. "It looks like our place in Oregon is going to sell. With the money from that, we'll have enough to put a down payment on the farm and buy a little equipment to get started. Maybe we can buy a cow, too. If we have some tough years, we'll have more variety on the table. For instance, Mom can make butter and cottage cheese."

"And ice cream," Emma added with a grin.

"And whipped cream," Frank said.

"Then we won't ever get to go back home?" I asked.

"Home?" Dad asked.

"Yeah, our home in the woods."

"No, if it sells, it won't be ours anymore. Our new farm will be our home." Dad glanced at Mom. "Are you terribly busy this afternoon? Could we take a ride?"

Mom smiled. "Sure."

"We have a farm in mind," Dad said. "We've applied for it, but we don't know yet whether or not we'll get it. Anyone want to go look at it?"

After dinner we climbed into the pickup and drove toward town. On our trips to and from school, we'd watched as new east–west roads had been built to intersect with Taylor-Flats Road, our usual route.

"Hey," Frank spoke above the banter as we drove toward our maybe-farm, "there's a road sign up. 'Fir Road.'"

We passed Dogwood, Cedar, and Birch Roads and turned left on Alder. "Who in the world came up with the road names?" Frank asked. "There's not a tree in sight!"

Several of us snickered as we scanned the treeless horizon.

Mom laughed. "Maybe someone's optimistic."

Emma sighed. "Or lonesome for trees."

Frank chuckled. "Or maybe it was the same person who put up the 'Keep Washington Green' sign between Umatilla and Wallula Junction."

Mom snickered.

119

The memories and the treeless view out the windows brought on a round of laughter.

We passed more desert and a couple green fields. Several miles later, we turned right onto another gravel road through desert. Half a mile farther we drove over a slight rise. Dad stopped the pickup and pointed. "There it is, on the right." His voice sounded happy. "Because of the canal angling across the north side, it's not a perfect square quarter section like a lot of the pieces, but it's still 160 acres. This triangle on the north corner will make a good pasture for the animals."

Dad drove down the ditch rider's road beside the canal—the gravel road for the man who cleared tumbleweeds out of the canal every spring, took the orders for water, and opened the headgates to give farmers the water they needed.

Dad angled the pickup onto the desert, then stopped. We walked around. "Seems like right here would be a good place to put the shack," Dad said.

Mom wandered slightly to the east. "The garden could go here."

We traipsed farther south. "There's a tiny hill!" I said. "At least it's not as flat as Uncle Max's place." It was hardly high enough to call a hill, but at least there was a short, slight slope to the south.

We noted the high-voltage power lines running through the corner of the property and the road alongside. "They'll be a bit of a nuisance," Dad said, "but we can farm around them."

We wandered over the sand and cheatgrass. There was less sagebrush here than there had been at Max's place when we'd arrived there. I got sandburs in my socks. Shortly, we crawled into the pickup and headed back to Max's farm. "The soil classification is worse here than it is at Max's," Dad said, "which means it's even sandier."

I didn't know soil could get sandier unless it would be at the beach . . . and nobody tried to farm there.

Mom and Dad filled out more paperwork. Talk of our own farm filled many table conversations.

"What will happen to Uncle Max's farm?"

"He'll move here and farm it himself."

Or

"Have you heard yet if the people for sure want to buy our place in Oregon?"

"No. It's not a done deal yet."

Or

"What will we do if we don't get a farm?"

"Where will we live if we don't get a farm?"

"When will we know?"

Suspense grew as spring warmed. Question followed question. There were way more questions than answers. But one question was uppermost—Will we get *our* farm?

CHAPTER 21

Where's Home?

That spring, school continued. My teacher reminded me frequently to speak louder. Mom used some of the flour from the Christmas box when she baked. The rye bread was lighter—in both color and weight. It looked more appetizing and made better-tasting sandwiches.

One spring day a tabby cat wandered in. It rubbed against my legs. When I petted it, it purred as loud as the engine from the tractor out in the field. I picked up the cat and carried it to the house. "Mom, we have a kitty!"

Mom took one look at the cat. "Probably someone dropped her off at the road," she said. "She has a very round middle. I'll bet she's about to have kittens."

Within days the addition to our family appropriated the name Mama Kitty. She proved to be a devoted mother to her five little balls of fur.

"I think we'll keep the cat," Dad announced one morning.

There were plenty of questions keeping us on edge lately, but in my mind, there'd never been a doubt about Mama Kitty staying.

"She's a wonderful hunter," Dad continued. "I've seen her with several mice. She'll be an asset."

Mama Kitty didn't romp with me as our big, woolly Smokey dog had done, but she became Hazel's and my friend in her own quiet way. She let us dress her in doll clothes. Then she sat on a chair with her tail hanging over the back of the seat. She listened to me tell Bible stories and teach the math I was learning at school. She was a patient student, but eventually she hopped off the chair and wandered away. Hazel or I ran after her and removed the dress and bonnet, so she'd not drag them through the sand and stickers.

One afternoon after school, Dad held up an official-looking big envelope. "This came in the mail today. Want to know what it says?"

Frank grinned. "Is it about the farm?"

"Yep!" Dad smiled. His eyes sparkled. "Our application to buy the farm we looked at has been approved."

"When do we move?" Frank asked.

"Not till summer. Besides, there's more paperwork to do, and we still have to get the money from our place in Oregon."

"If we get the money," Emma asked, "won't we have to move out the piano and the other furniture that's still there?"

"Yep, we will."

Emma's brows furrowed. "What are we going to do with it?"

Dad sighed. "Don't know yet."

"We can't just set the furniture out in the middle of the desert to fill up with sand!"

"You're right," Dad said. "And we won't."

Dad shelled out a dime for a newspaper from time to time and looked at ads for farm equipment. He purchased a used blade for behind the tractor. "We'll need this on our farm," he said. Dad also went to farm implement dealers and asked lots of questions. He studied and shopped for irrigation pumps and equipment.

One evening, he had a different kind of news. "I was going to look at something on our new farm, when I noticed action at another place. I stopped and asked for the owner. The man said, 'The owners don't live here, but I'm the manager. Can I help you?' So I said, 'I was wondering if you are going to be hiring any hands.' He answered, 'Matter of fact, we are. What do you have in mind?' I told him we'd farmed on my brother's place up in Block 15 for two years and would be moving onto our own farm in Block 16, just a couple miles north from there, and I would like a job. He asked a lot of questions about what I'd done before we moved there, my experience driving equipment, and what I knew about building and mechanics. The last question he asked was, 'When can you go to work?'"

"So you got the job?" Frank asked. "What will you be doing? Who are you working for?"

"Glade Farms. I'll help them start up their farm—including building a shop. They'll be planting alfalfa soon. I'll help plant and change sprinklers. When the hay's big enough I'll mow it, rake it, and bale it. If they have mechanical things I can do, I'll help with that. I'll do anything a farmer does."

Dad grinned and chuckled. "Except there's one big difference," he said. "I'll get paid before the end of the year. And I'll get paid whether or not the farm makes any money."

Mom giggled. "That will be a nice change."

"Can we get some toilet paper?" Emma asked. "There aren't many pages left in the catalog."

"Hold on," Dad said. "I haven't even gone to work yet. And a pay-check's further down the road. Besides, it won't be a regular nine-to-five job. I'll only work when they need me, so we can't depend on a regular paycheck of a certain amount."

Over the next few weeks, Dad went to work at Glade Farms, the school year ended, and we got word that as soon as we got our furniture out of our house in Oregon, the buyers would give us the small amount Dad and Mom had agreed to accept as full payment. But where would we put our piano and furniture?

Dad enjoyed his work at Glade Farms. Carl Meier, the manager, appreciated that Dad had a variety of skills—he could do manual labor, run equipment, build, weld, or do electrical and plumbing. He could help pour foundations for the three cabins they would move there to house workers. He didn't complain if it was 95 degrees and the job at hand was shoveling. He showed up for work when he said he would, and, unlike some of the other workers, he never arrived drunk. Carl was also amazed at Dad and Mom's plans to move back with their family into an 8-by-16-foot shack, at their willingness to endure short-term hardship for a long-term goal.

We still lived in the shop at Uncle Max's place, but on our new farm, the power company put in poles and wire to get electricity to where we planned to put the shack and a little farther west to where we would install an irrigation pump. Since Glade Farms would need to call Dad about work, the telephone company put in a phone line. "That's not money spent," Mom said. "It's an investment that will pay for itself."

When Dad had several hours or a day off work, he and Frank loaded the tractor and plow onto the truck. Then they loaded whatever lumber wasn't being used—such as the lean-to planks that had been over Emma's and my bed outside the shack. They built a pen for the sheep and goats.

Dad borrowed a trailer, and they dedicated a day to sliding the shack onto the trailer with chains and binders—a method they called "walking the dog." Slowly, as they tightened a binder, moved it, and tightened it again and again, one end of the shack slid up some boards and onto the trailer.

It was hard work on a hot day on the black pavement. Several times I carried glasses and a pitcher of water to them. Frank even seemed happy to see his kid sister in those moments. Over and over again, they worked the binders and the shack slid lengthwise until it sat on the trailer. The next day they hauled it to our new farm and unloaded it. I didn't go along, but they took lunches . . . and lots of drinking water.

The buyers of our house and acreage in Oregon were getting eager to finish the deal and move in.

After work one day, Dad said, "I told Carl today that I was going to need to take a few days off to go get our things from our house in Oregon. I asked him when would be the best time for me to be gone. After we talked about times, Carl asked, 'How much stuff do you have?' I said, 'A piano, a few pieces of furniture, and a bunch of boxes.' He asked, 'What are you going to do with them when you get them here?' I said, 'I don't know, but I sure need to be finding out.'"

Dad paused, grinned, then continued. "Carl pointed over at the last helper's house and said, 'We put in these houses for workers. You're one of our workers. Since you'll be living nearby, you don't need to live in it. But I see no reason in the world why you can't store your things there.'"

Mom smiled. "So we have a place out of the weather for our things."

"Yep!" Dad chuckled. "And we can get things when we need them or take stuff back to store there."

I grinned. "Could I play the piano when we go there?"

"I imagine that would be just fine." Dad cleared his throat. "So now that that's settled, can we go after our things the first of next week?"

Dad made arrangements for a neighbor to care for the animals. Mom packed the picnic basket full.

"Can I ride in the back?" Frank asked. "It'll be cooler."

"And it'll be more pleasant in the cab," Emma added.

Dad grinned. "Yep. You may."

The drive in the big truck seemed to take forever. As on earlier trips, we stopped at Celilo Falls for lunch. "Enjoy the view," Dad said, "and the sound of the falls. A dam is being built downstream and this will all be flooded."

Water cascaded over rocks across the broad Columbia River. In one place, the river narrowed. Water roared between rock walls, dropping into violent turbulence. Again, various fishermen with spears and nets mounted on long poles fished for salmon. As we drove on, Dad pointed out where The Dalles dam was being built.

Finally, the air cooled near Portland. At McMinnville the locale began to feel familiar. Then Sheridan . . . Willamina . . . onto the gravel road . . . Willamina Creek. I breathed deep of the forest fragrance. My heart beat faster.

We passed a driveway on the left that wound up a hill. I turned, looked out the back window, and spotted the familiar white building with its steeple. "There's our church!" Then we passed the next road to the left that wandered down the valley to the school and gym.

We drove up the familiar hill. It almost felt like everyone in the cab of the truck was holding their breath. Then, there it was—our house. We were home!

Except . . . it *wasn't* home.

CHAPTER 22

Mom Didn't Look Back

Frank pounded on the back window. "There's our house!" he yelled.

As if the rest of us don't know it! I thought, but I was too excited to chance irking my brother at this electric moment.

In one sense, the house looked beautiful! But it didn't look right. There were no red geraniums in the flower boxes contrasting against the white walls. The lawn was overgrown. Mom's garden plot was filled with tall weeds. Smokey wasn't there to greet us with a deep woof and wagging tail.

Still, there was much to see. The waterfall. I'd always loved the waterfall, but after two years in the desert, I stood in awe, gazing at water cascading over the cliff. And the wild strawberries on the back hillside—were they red and ready to eat? No.

Then the house. Mom's dream house. She had helped plan it. Dad had built it, with some help from Mom's brother and brother-in-law. From a cabin at the top of the hill, Mom had watched the building progress. Then the move. She had loved her life in that house. She had loved her life in that community, full of relatives and friends.

Mom never complained, but she couldn't have felt the same about her life in the desert. After a year sleeping outside and a year living in a shop, Mom stepped softly around the nicest house she'd ever lived in, almost as if it was sacred space.

To me, the house felt familiar and odd all at once. The kitchen— Emma turned the faucet. "Running water!" she exclaimed. The living room—where Emma and Frank had practiced the piano whether or not they wanted to, where I had watched and longed for the day when I could take piano lessons, too, and learn to make music, where Dad had read aloud so many stories and whole books to us through long winter evenings. The bedrooms—without beds they looked lonely. The bathroom—with a real bathtub and a flush toilet! The basement—where scores of jars of canned fruit and veg-etables used to fill long shelves, where we heated the house with a wood furnace, where we washed the clothes and never had to worry about a wash tub blowing to the next state. The house felt lonely.

By the next day, it looked lonelier. The house was totally empty. The garage was empty. The truck was full.

Dad and Frank finished tying down the load. Dad came into the house. "If you want a last look around," he said, "now's the time."

We wandered through the empty house. I dreaded walking out the door. Saying goodbye to our house made me want to cry.

I walked behind the house. Double-checked to see if any of the scrumptious, tiny wild strawberries had ripened. They hadn't. I gazed at the waterfall. I breathed deep of the forest fragrance. The rest of the family joined me. We stood, silent in the forest except for bird song from the trees and the sound of water rushing over rocks.

Dad finally broke the spell. "If we're going to get *there*," he said, "we have to leave *here*."

One by one, we silently turned and walked toward the truck. "Everyone in the cab," Dad said.

"I'd sure rather ride in the back like I did on the way here," Frank said.

"But there's no place to sit back there now."

All six of us squeezed onto the one truck seat—Dad at the steering wheel. Mom beside him, holding almost-three-year-old Hazel. Next to Mom, Frank leaned against the back of the seat. Emma sat by the passenger door, and I perched on the front edge of the seat between my two older siblings' legs.

Dad glanced in the rearview mirror as we started to move, then smiled as he looked at the road ahead. Emma and Frank craned their necks backward. I leaned across Emma and looked out the side window to get a last glimpse of home.

"We've had some hard times the last couple years," Dad said, "but it's bound to get better."

Mom didn't look back. She looked straight ahead . . . her jaw set. Tears silently slid down her cheeks.

CHAPTER 23

Moving

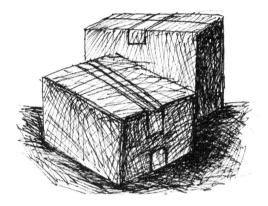

Our truck carried the final load of our family's belongings. Three hundred miles hadn't gotten any shorter. Dad told story after story. Mom, always a quiet soul, was way more quiet than usual.

The day wore on.

"Frank," I whined, "quit pushing me off the seat!"

"I can't help it!" he complained. "I've got to wiggle once in a while."

"My back is tired!" I grumbled.

"Frank," Mom said, "why don't you scoot up and let Helen move back so she can lean on the seatback for a while."

Frank scooted forward and I scrunched back. It felt wonderful to rest my back.

Dad started singing, "Row, row, row your boat," then broke in, "Come on, kids, join in."

Row, row, row, your boat, gently down the stream.
Merrily, merrily, merrily, merrily, life is but a dream.

We sang in rounds—Dad led the first part and Mom and us kids chimed in with the second part. When we got to "Life is but a dream," Mom quit singing and got a funny look on her face.

The rest of us sang one song, then another:

> There were ten in the bed and the little one said, 'Roll over, roll over.'
> So they all rolled over and one fell out.
> There were nine in the bed and the little one said, 'Roll over, roll over.'
> So they all rolled over and one fell out.
> There were eight in the bed and the little one said . . .

We sang on and on.

> There were two in the bed and the little one said, 'Roll over, roll over.'
> So they all rolled over and one fell out.
> There was one in the bed and the little one said, 'Goodnight! Goodnight!'

Memories stirred. We'd often sung together on our frequent Saturday night fifteen-mile jaunts to Papa and Grandmommy's. Now Grandmommy was gone and Papa had sold the farm and moved into an apartment in town. We wouldn't be able to go to their farm ever again . . . or to our home in the woods. Even though all six of us were scrunched together closer than any of us really wanted to be, I felt an empty, lonely spot in my heart.

As the miles and hours passed, Dad told more stories about growing up on his grandpa and grandma's farm in southern Idaho. Emma, Frank, and I traded positions from time to time. Different ones held Hazel.

Several of Dad's stories were about the wise old horse he rode to school every day.

"Can I have a horse?" I asked.

"Not now," Dad answered. "Money's still going to be tight for a while."

We stopped at Glade Farms. Dad backed up the truck to the worker's cabin where his boss had agreed to let us store things. We unloaded the piano, furniture, and many boxes, then drove a couple miles farther to the farm to which we would soon move. There we unloaded the tools and miscellany that we'd taken out of the garage at our Oregon home.

Since Glade Farms didn't need Dad immediately, the next day became moving day. First thing after breakfast, Frank and Dad loaded the animals in the truck and drove them to their new abode. Mom had already packed some boxes. She and Emma took down the curtain "walls" between our sleeping "rooms." I watched Hazel and helped fold blankets. Then we packed more boxes, keeping out enough food for dinner. In the last load, the outhouse stood on the truck and Mama Kitty and her brood meowed from a box on my lap.

By nightfall, we lived on our own farm. This time the shack door faced west. The kitchen was back in the shack and, lying in bed, we looked up at the stars again. But there was something new here. As I watched the stars glisten across the night sky, I heard a whistle—faint, but clear.

"Are we near railroad tracks?" I called.

"Only a couple miles away," Dad answered through the dark.

I lay there, listening for more train whistles, looking up at the sparkle of the Big Dipper, Orion, and a million stars glistening across the Milky Way, and wondering . . . wondering if anything would change. Wondering . . . *will things ever get better?*

CHAPTER 24

Starting Over

First thing the first morning on our new farm Mom said, "Wayne, while I fix breakfast, would you take the older kids out and explain about the canal?"

Emma, Frank, and I followed Dad through the stickery tumbleweeds and stood on the ditch rider's road. On our farm the canal was closer to the shack than it had been at Max's place. "We want you guys to respect this canal," Dad said. He pointed. "See how fast the water goes down into that culvert?"

"Yeah," we answered in near-unison.

"If someone got caught and pulled into it, I don't know if they'd make it out the other end alive. But that's only part of the problem." He waved for us to follow.

We crossed the gravel road and looked down at water whirling in a small pool about eight feet across. He pointed back across the road, then down at the pool beside us. "The water from over there," he said, "comes out here."

"Yeah?"

"Then it goes into this culvert and drops down there." He pointed across the sand about twenty feet.

We followed him down to the continuation of the canal. "If someone small—like Hazel—ended up going through one of these culverts, she probably wouldn't live to tell about it. And, even if she survived until she got here, she wouldn't be able to pull herself out of this whirlpool."

We gazed at the swirling water.

"This is dangerous!" Dad emphasized. "You guys, just stay away from the canal! Got that?"

"Uh-huh."

Emma's eyebrows furrowed. "But where are we going to bathe?"

"We'll soon have a sump," Dad said. "No one will need to go near the canal." He looked at one, then another. "Always, *always* stay far away from the culverts! And all of us need to keep an eye on Hazel! Don't let her get anywhere near here. It would be too easy for her to fall in."

Keeping an eye on Hazel, however, was getting harder. At nearly three years old, her speed had increased dramatically, and the canal here was much closer. It did help, however, that in the summer she usually had bare legs and tumbleweeds filled the space between the shack and canal. Their stickers would help keep her corralled.

Ah-h-h, the first positive thought I'd had about the miserable, stickery tumbleweeds! Even though I liked to sing *Tumbling Tumbleweeds* along with the Sons of the Pioneers on the radio, until that moment, I had seen no earthly good for tumbleweeds.

After breakfast, Dad showed Frank where to dig a shallow ditch for burying a small pipe from where the irrigation pump would be to Mom's proposed garden site. Frank set to work with a shovel.

Mom came out of the shack with a pitcher, pulled the lid off the ten-gallon water can by the door, and tipped it. She looked up at Dad. "We're getting low on drinking water," she said. "Any chance you could get some this morning before you head out to the field?"

"Yep. Can do it right now." He poured the last of the water into Mom's pitcher, then loaded the five-gallon and ten-gallon cans into the pickup. "It's a little farther to the well house here than it was up at Max's, but only about three miles. Shouldn't take long . . . unless there's a line of others getting water too."

When Dad returned, he hooked the blade behind the tractor, headed to the northeast corner of our farm, and started digging a ditch for irrigation water.

At supper he explained, "I got the ditch dug from the canal to where we'll dig a sump."

"What's a sump?" I asked.

"A reservoir."

I wrinkled my forehead.

"A pond," he said. "We can only take a certain amount of water out of the canal at a time, and sometimes we might need more water than we can get right then. So we'll dig a sump—a pond—so we can store irrigation water there and have it whenever we need it to water our crops."

Within a couple days, Dad showed us the sump. It was shaped like a long vee, about ten feet deep in the center and sloping up to each side. It was about twenty feet wide and thirty feet long. The dirt dug out of the middle was stacked on each side making the banks higher than the surrounding sand.

"Can we go swimming tomorrow?" Frank asked.

"And have a bath?" Emma added.

"Whoa . . . not so fast," Dad answered. "I've got to order water yet, and the ditch rider may not be able to open the headgate on the same day—other farmers need water too."

"What's a headgate?" I asked.

Dad pointed to the corner where he'd started digging the ditch. "It's a gate the ditch rider can open or close to let water from the canal flow into our ditch." He cleared his throat. "As for swimming, even after the water is turned on, it'll take a while—at first, a lot of water will soak into the dry sand on its way toward the sump. And a lot will soak into the sump as it fills up, too. But after the water soaks in, the ditch and sump will hold water. Our big bathtub will fill up within a few days. I'll put our order for water up by the head-gate tonight."

That evening, Dad and Frank lay small pipe—about an inch in diameter—in the ditch Frank had dug. They installed a faucet near the garden site. No water, but we had a faucet. There was hope.

The next morning before Dad headed to his job, he attached the plow behind the tractor and plowed once around a square area south of the shack. "We'll start with this," he told Frank. He looked out over the field. "It's about . . . uh-h-h . . . twenty acres. After we get this field plowed and planted, we'll start another field."

Frank climbed on the tractor and started plowing, Dad went to his job. Emma covered the pipe to the garden with a little unpro-fessional help from Hazel and me, and Mom pulled out packets of vegetable seeds and started making plans.

Within a few days, irrigation water filled the sump. We took soap along when we went for a swim. Cool water—what a refreshing relief from the heat! Getting clean felt great too!

When morning came, Frank went back to plowing. That evening after he finished plowing the field, Mom asked Dad, "Would this be a good time to plow the garden spot? If we're going to have vegeta-bles, we need to get them planted."

"Sure thing," Dad said. He gave Frank a break and plowed the garden spot himself.

"Garden's ready," he told Mom.

"Thanks," Mom said.

Dad turned to Frank. "Shall we manufacture a new piece of equipment?"

"What?" Frank asked.

"Well, I not only learned that sprinklers do a better job in this country than corrugations, it's also really clear that, especially when we're going to plant a crop that lasts several years, it will work better if we can smooth the field."

"So what are we making?" Frank asked.

"How about if I show you," Dad answered.

He and Frank cobbled together a plank with weights on it. Frank pulled it behind the tractor over the plowed field and it smoothed the ground. When he drove the tractor to the shack, Dad pushed his hat back and surveyed the field. "Looks lots better!" he said. "It's ready to plant. Let's get the pump set up."

Dad set the irrigation pump in its place by the sump and hooked it to electricity. A truck and trailer came bringing lots of aluminum pipes. Most of the pipes were 4 inches in diameter, 40 feet long, and on one end had a riser—a skinny pipe with a sprinkler on top. "Those are the hand lines," Dad explained. "We'll hook the individual pipes together and string them out in a long row the length of the field. There are enough pipes for two lines. We'll start using them as soon as we get the field planted."

A couple pipes were only half as long. "How come these are so short?" I asked.

"Those go at the beginning of each line," Dad explained. "To make sure that the beginning of the field gets all the water it needs."

Some pipes were bigger around. They were six inches in diameter, thirty feet long, and had a strange looking contraption on one end instead of a sprinkler. "What are these bigger pipes?" I asked.

"Those are main line pipes."

"What . . ."

"Well, Miss Question Box," Dad interrupted, "how about if tomorrow we show you how they work rather than trying to explain it now?"

The next morning, Dad drove the tractor to work.

"I'm going to load the main line pipes," Frank told Mom, "so they'll be ready when Dad gets home." He headed outside and loaded the largest pipes onto the pipe trailer Dad had built.

Late that morning, Dad came home towing a contraption on rubber tires that was wider than the tractor, but not very long. A row of boxes sat at the top. He stopped in a corner of the plowed field and came in for lunch.

"I'm grateful the boss likes my work!" he said. "He says he wishes he could pay me more, but since he can't, maybe loaning us some equipment once in a while will make up for it."

"That's been a major blessing!" Mom said.

"So," Emma asked, "what's the thing you towed home today?"

"A drill," Dad answered.

"A drill?" There was puzzlement in Emma's voice. "Doesn't look like anything you'd drill holes with."

Dad leaned back in his chair and laughed softly. "No, not that kind of drill," he said. "It's a seeding drill. You dump seed in the metal boxes on top. The seed slowly runs down the tubes beneath the boxes. Did you notice the little metal plates at the bottom?"

"No."

"They go just below the surface of the ground and plant the seeds in narrow rows. Maybe that's how it got its name—it drills down into the ground."

After lunch Dad drove the pickup down the road to the edge of the field, next to the drill. Frank carried some of the bags of alfalfa seed from the pickup, and he and Dad filled the seed boxes on the drill. Then Dad pulled the drill behind the tractor, planting tiny alfalfa seeds in rows only a couple inches apart. He stopped and checked the drill once in a while. When he whistled and waved, Frank drove the pickup to the tractor and they refilled the drill's seed boxes.

When he finished planting, Dad drove the tractor to the shack. "I'm hot and thirsty," he said. "Just like that field is. Soon as I get a drink, let's string out the pipes."

Frank disconnected the tractor from the drill, then connected it to the pipe trailer. Emma drove the tractor along the west edge of the field, stopping for Dad and Frank each to get a thirty-foot-long pipe and fasten it in a long line to the previous pipe. They ended the line of pipes with a plug.

"Now that we have the main line in place," Dad said, "it's time for the sprinkler lines."

Emma drove back to the farmyard and pulled the trailer alongside the pile of smaller-diameter pipes. Frank loaded pipe after pipe, then the three headed back to the field. At the south edge of the field farthest from the shack, they added an opener on a valve on the main line and hooked and latched the twenty-foot pipe to it. Next, they strung together one forty-foot pipe after another—each with a riser and sprinkler—until they came to the end of the field. They plugged the end of the line.

With one sprinkler line in a row, they came to the side of the field closest to the shack and strung out another line of sprinklers.

"The proof's in the pudding," Dad said. "Let's see if it all works."

Hazel and I followed Dad to the sump. He started the water pump. It purred. I looked to where they'd just strung out the line of sprinkler pipes. "Nothing's happening," I said.

"Water's working its way down the main line," Dad said. "Keep watching."

Shortly, the sprinkler heads started spinning in circles. Air whooshed from them. Droplets of water spit from one, then the next.

"It's working!" Dad said.

"There's not much water coming out."

"Give it a minute. The water has to push all the air out of the pipes and build up pressure before the sprinklers work well."

Sure enough, shortly the sprinklers each swished irrigation water in a slow circle that reached to the next sprinkler.

"The ground is going to need to be kept damp," Dad said at supper. He looked at Frank. "So, we'll let both lines run while we eat. Then it's back to the races. For the first few days, you'll need to move one line over to the next opener, then move the other. Just keep doing that—back and forth. When they meet in the middle, carry them back to their starting points and start over again."

"All day?" Frank asked.

"You can have breaks for meals," Dad said.

Frank sighed.

"We've all worked hard," Dad said. "And besides pump and sprinklers, we've spent money on fuel and seed. But if we don't keep the field damp and a wind comes up . . ." He paused.

Frank jumped in. "The seed could all blow away again, huh?"

"Yep."

"And all the work and money would be wasted."

"Yep."

CHAPTER 25

If Only . . .

After supper, Frank headed out to change sprinklers. He turned off the water at the valve on the main line and carried the opener the thirty feet to the next valve. Then he toted the first pipe and reconnected it to the valve. One by one, he carried each pipe to the next setting and reconnected it. When he got to the end of the row, he walked back to the beginning and turned the opener. Air hissed out of the sprinklers, then water. He wiped his forehead and headed for the other line of sprinklers.

By dark, Frank was glad to quit and come in for worship and bed. "Please help the wind not to blow tonight," several prayed.

First thing the next morning, Frank changed both lines—about an hour's work. At breakfast he said, "The sprinklers are almost across the field the first time—only a couple changes left."

"And no hard winds so far!" Mom exclaimed. "Maybe this crop will be okay."

"Hopefully the calm will last a little longer," Dad added. He looked up at Emma. "How about if you help change sprinklers today?"

"I don't know if I can lift the pipes."

"They're not heavy. But they are awkward." He furrowed his brows a moment, then looked at me. "Helen, you go along and help Emma. You can carry the light end."

After breakfast, I joined the irrigation crew. I carried the light end of each pipe and set it in place. From the far end of the pipe, Emma pushed the pipe in, turned it, and pulled to latch it. The sun beat down on us. The air was calm—a blessing to the field, a trial to our comfort. Between lines we took enough break to wipe the sweat off our brows, get drinks of water, and make a trip to the outhouse.

After the two sprinkler lines met in the middle and dampened the dust there, Frank carried the south line—one pipe at a time—all the way back to the south edge of the field. Emma and I carried our line all the way to the north edge of the field. Both lines were right back where they had started, but the whole field had been watered once.

Shortly before lunch, after changing several lines, Emma said, "I think I can do this. Let me try it on my own." She went to the middle of a pipe, disconnected it from the pipe further on, then lifted one end to drain out the water. She balanced the pipe and carried it to the next position, lowered the latch end into the previous pipe, pushed, turned, and pulled. Pipe after pipe she managed without my help. Suddenly I was out of an irrigation job and back to full-time Hazel-watcher and Mom-helper.

"Now that there's irrigation water," Mom said, "it's time to plant the garden."

We planted radishes, carrots, string beans, and a host of other vegetables. Mom connected a hose to the faucet Dad and Frank had put in earlier. With the turn of a knob, the garden had running water. Yay! Too bad the irrigation water wasn't clean enough to drink.

The community well where we got drinking water was about three miles from our farm, near the ditch rider's home. We could go anytime to get drinking water, but sometimes we had to wait in line. More and more farmers were moving into the area, and few had their own wells. Some people came, like we did, to fill a few small five-gallon and ten-gallon cans. Others had large tanks on the back of trucks, so we never knew how long it would take to wait our turn.

We couldn't see neighbors in any direction from our place, but we passed two different farms on the way to the well house. Waiting for water was a good time to meet new neighbors.

At home, there wasn't half a chance that *anyone* would get bored. Mom and I watched Hazel, cooked meals, ground the wheat Mom had purchased, baked bread, and moved the garden hose and sprinkler so every row got watered. All of us kids got in on washing and drying dishes—with a family of six, there were plenty. Serving dishes nearly always added to the accumulation. Nothing had changed—not only must the table be set correctly, the only time a kettle was allowed on the table was for breakfast cereal. After all, according to Mom, we were a civilized family.

And that was just the housework. The church needed to be cleaned every Thursday. Every morning and evening the animals needed to be fed, watered, and milked. Hour after hour, the sprinklers needed to be changed. And Frank still found energy to tease the ram—from outside the fence—and laugh at the creature's frustration.

As the days passed, fragile green shoots in tiny rows poked through the sand, grew pairs of leaves, then more leaves.

"Hey, you honyocks," Dad said at breakfast one morning, "how would you like a break between sprinkler moves?"

Frank nodded. "Uh-huh," he voiced through a mouthful of oatmeal.

"Yeah!" Emma agreed.

"The plants are strong enough now that you can grab a rest between changes. We still need to move each line every two hours, but that will give you a break between."

Frank and Emma both smiled.

"Of course, we wouldn't want you to get bored." Dad grinned.

Emma raised an eyebrow. Frank groaned and looked out of the corner of his eye at Dad.

"Now that the alfalfa's growing, it's time to start plowing another field."

That afternoon Dad made one trip around another plot of desert grass on the far side of the irrigation main line, then Frank took over the plowing for the next few days. From time to time, he'd stop and change sprinklers to give Emma a break. When that field was plowed, Frank smoothed the ground with the homemade device. Then after work at Glade Farms one afternoon, Dad planted wheat across the new field. One pipe at a time, Frank and Emma carried one line of sprinklers from the alfalfa field to the wheat field. Time to water a new crop.

Dad also introduced us to a new project that filled any spare moments between sprinkler changing and other chores—digging a cellar. He put stakes at the four corners and tied strings between them to show us the perimeter. The shovel was available to whoever had time. We all got in on the digging, some more productively than others. Even Hazel used her plastic toy bucket and shovel. Slowly, day by day, the hole grew deeper and the pile of sand beside the hole grew higher.

The summer temperatures at our farm were as hot as they had been at Max's. Digging was hard and hot work. And that summer there was hardly a breeze. Though a blessing to the growing plants, we could have appreciated a light breeze.

But we had the sump. We bathed in it. And it was deep enough and big enough that we could swim in it, too. That deep of a bathtub had one disadvantage, however—when we dropped a bar of soap in the canal by Uncle Max's place, we could just feel around and find it. When we dropped a bar of soap in the sump, we could look for it, feel for it, dive for it, but sometimes never find it.

The sun bore down. The sprinklers dampened the sand. The green in the alfalfa field grew thicker.

Some days Dad took the truck and went to equipment auctions. In due time he came home with both an old mower and rake to attach to the tractor. "We'll need these before long," he said. "Have you seen how green the alfalfa field is looking?"

"Yes, I have," Mom said. "And how is the wheat doing?"

"It's starting to come up. If only the wind will stay calm until the alfalfa and wheat plants are big enough to withstand blowing sand. If only . . ."

CHAPTER 26

Progress

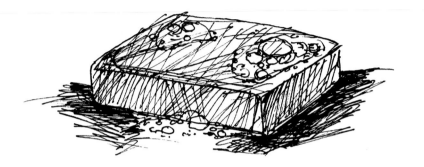

Shortly after we moved, Uncle Max and his family moved from their western Oregon home to their farm—where we'd lived the last two years. At least an uncle, an aunt, and one cousin lived near us again.

One day, Dad and Frank put racks on the truck bed, then drove away in a cloud of dust. Later they arrived back home accompanied by unusual sounds—mooing. "She's a Guernsey," Dad said. "Supposed to be calm and an easy-milker. She should give plenty of milk for our family."

"No more goat milk?" Emma asked.

"Can't promise," Dad said, "but, with Bossie, there's a pretty good chance."

Bossie joined the sheep and goats in their corral. That evening Dad milked her. He brought in a large bucket full of frothing milk. Mom strained it, filled several clear glass jars, and put the milk in the refrigerator. The next morning when she placed a jar of Bossie's milk on the table, I stared at it. "How come the top of the milk looks different than the bottom?"

"Cow's milk has more cream than goat milk." Mom pointed to the line in the jar where the color changed. "The cream rose to the top. We'll have cream on our mush this morning."

The cream tasted rich on our oatmeal.

Bossie proved to be a gentle soul. She never kicked when she was milked, unless something startled her. Still, the morning and evening chores expanded. Dad, Frank, and Emma all got in on milking her.

Other projects progressed, too. Shovelful by shovelful, the hole for the cellar finally grew to 6 feet wide, 12 feet long, and 4 feet deep.

Near the southwest corner, Dad built a wooden frame and steps down into the hole. Over the hole, he built a plywood roof slanted high enough that adults could stand straight in the middle. In the roof, he left space for a door above the stairs. Above a thick door-frame, he added a plywood door at the same angle as the roof. Inside the cellar, he built shelves on one side for the hundreds of jars of fruit and vegetables Mom would preserve.

"Ready for a cool place to sleep?" Dad asked Frank.

"More than ready!"

They took Frank's bed apart, moved it into the cellar, and set it up across from the shelves.

But the cellar wasn't finished yet. We spread some of the straw we had for the animals across the roof, then shoveled over the straw the sand we'd previously dug out of the cellar hole. "For insulation," Dad said. After we covered the straw with sand, Dad set the garden sprinkler to run on it, "To pack it down," he explained, "so it won't blow away in the first breeze." Then we added more straw, more sand, and more water.

"With the straw and sand over the roof," Dad said, "the cellar will definitely be cooler in summer and warmer in winter."

Frank had the luxury suite again—even an electric light bulb. The coolness had to feel wonderful on a hot evening, but before long, he shared his quarters with hordes of uninvited guests—spiders and their fly-filled webs. That took the glamour out of "luxury."

Life for Frank, however, involved more than cool nights for sleeping. One afternoon when Dad came home from working at Glade Farms, he asked, "Frank, would you like to make some money?"

"What doing?"

"Bucking bales."

"You bet. Where?"

"Glade Farms. We're starting to bale the first crop of hay. They have a truck and an elevator, but they need someone to haul and stack the bales."

"But we need two people," Frank said. "Do they have someone else?"

"Not yet. Do you know anyone who might be able to handle the job?"

"Hm-m-m." Frank thought a moment. "Yeah!" he said. "Dale's pretty stout. I think he could handle it. I'll telephone him." He headed for the phone on the wall just inside the shack door.

So Frank and Dale started their bale-bucking career. Each morning Frank ran to work—about two miles. Dale drove from town and met him there. They started at four o'clock most mornings so they could get caught up with the baled hay before the heat of day. They got paid by the bale—extra incentive to work hard! Throwing hundred-pound bales of hay around was hard work for a couple teen boys who didn't weigh much more than the bales. Daily, Frank's lunch included sandwiches from a whole loaf of Mom's home-baked, whole-wheat bread.

With Frank gone to work, Emma got the brunt of changing sprinklers every two hours . . . day after day. And feeding and watering the animals and milking the cow and goats. I was glad I was considered too young for milking the cow—I definitely was not fond of the fragrance she contributed to whoever leaned their head against her side while they milked her or . . . accidentally stepped in her cow pies. Frank helped in the afternoon after he got home from bucking bales. Their diligence paid off. The tiny alfalfa plants grew big enough that, instead of looking like tiny rows, the field looked like it was covered with a green carpet. Little green plants sprouted all over the wheat field too.

The heat helped the plants grow. It helped the humans wilt. "At least we can cool off in the sump," Mom said.

That we did—regularly. One afternoon when we donned swimming suits, the soap was white and looked like a new bar. We each grabbed our own washcloth and towel. At our super-sized bathtub, Emma walked into the water neck deep. She scrubbed her face and arms. "Oh, no," she muttered. "I dropped the soap." She took a deep breath. "Frank," she hollered, "will you come try to find the soap?"

"Just dive for it," he called, a smirk on his face.

"No. You know I hate to get my face wet! Please come get it!"

"Okay. Since you're a sissy," he taunted, "I'll come hunt for it." He swam toward Emma.

All of a sudden, Emma's eyes got big. "Forget it," she called.

"Why?"

"It's right here. It floated."

Frank was beside her at that point. "That's different," he said.

A scientific experiment began—they tried to get the soap to sink. Over and over it popped right back to the surface.

When we got clean and cool, we headed back to the shack. "Did you get a different kind of soap this time?"

"Yes," Mom said. "Ivory soap was on sale. Why?"

"It floats!" Emma said.

"Hm-m-m," Mom said. "Even if it's not on sale, it may be the cheapest soap to send to the sump."

Our afternoon swims were a cooling break, but they didn't stop work. After the cellar was complete, Dad began another building project—a 10 x 10-foot granary. Dad laid a 2 x 4 board down on the broad side and nailed on one 2 x 4 after another, alternating side to side which board went all the way to the corner. Slowly, all four walls grew, with space for a door in the middle of the west side. Finally, Dad added an aluminum peaked roof, a piece of canvas for a door, and a light bulb on a cord. For the time being, Emma's and my bedroom was complete. It didn't take long to move our bed and a chest of drawers into the granary.

We kids had makeshift shelter again. Mom and Dad still slept out in the elements.

Many nights, before I stepped into the granary, I looked up at the diamond-studded sky. After I crawled into bed, I lay there, listening to the stillness, and then the trains' whoooooo-hooo-hoooo. I even learned to enjoy the eerie coyote wails.

Occasionally, Mom needed to drive to Glade Farms to get something out of storage. "May I go?" I asked.

"I go?" a little voice chimed after me.

When we got there, I headed to the piano. On the first visit after we stored things there, Mom showed me where middle C was on the piano and in the beginner piano books. She showed me what notes on the different lines and spaces meant in the music. While Mom searched through various boxes for what she came after, I began to pick out musical phrases on the piano . . . along with Hazel dong, dong, donging bass notes.

Sometimes Mom opened up the treadle sewing machine and mended the latest rips or patched the latest holes. A couple times she made shirts for Hazel and me out of the printed, fabric flour bags.

Each opportunity to play the piano was a delight to me. On the way home one afternoon, Mom said, "You're doing well on the piano."

"Now that we have a piano, may I take piano lessons?" I asked. I watched Mom's face.

Her eyes darkened. "That won't work now," she said. "If you were taking lessons, you'd need to practice every day, and we can't bring you here to practice every day."

"But when will we get to have the piano at home?"

"I don't know," Mom said. "There's not room for it in the shack. We can't really have the piano until we have a house."

"When will we get a house?"

Mom took a deep breath. "I wish I knew when we could build a real house."

CHAPTER 27

Weeds

"The weeds north of the house are growing crazy fast," Dad said one evening. "We may as well build a fence around it and let our animals eat the weeds. It'll save money on feed and keep the weeds down, too."

So holes at corners and occasionally in between for wooden posts became the next project. After a few days, Dad and Frank pounded in metal posts between the wooden posts. They connected white ceramic insulators to each post and strung wire from insulator to insulator around the five-acre field at nose-height for the sheep and goats.

Hazel and I watched from nearby.

"There!" Dad said when they got one strand fastened in place. "Done with that project!" He and Frank started picking up tools and material.

"Aren't you going to put up more wire?" I asked. "One wire won't keep the critters in, will it?"

"It wouldn't if we were just counting on the wire, but it'll be an electric fence. The critters are apt to stick their moist noses out to sniff the wire, and the fence will give them a jolt they don't care for. We'll have to watch them at first, but after they get used to the fence, there shouldn't be a problem."

And so it happened. Dad hooked the wire up to an electric fence charger. "Don't touch the fence," he warned. "It won't care if it's a critter or if it's you. It'll shock anything that touches it." He paused, then added, "Hopefully you'll never experience this, but, if for some reason you grabbed hold of it, let go as soon as you can. The fence will give intermittent jolts," he explained. "Very quickly, it'll zap, then turn off, zap, turn off, zap . . . It's a safety thing." He turned to Frank, "Why don't you open the gate?"

The sheep and goats gathered near the open gate. The billy goat ventured through first. He started eating weeds. Looking curious, a couple sheep stepped through the gate. They nibbled a few weeds, then bounced in apparent delight and raced across the pasture. The rest of the animals followed. Shortly, most settled down to eating the abundant weeds. A few stuck out their noses toward the fence. They jumped back, eyes wide, staring at the thin wire. They apparently got zapped with an electric shock, just like Dad had said. A couple sheep tried the fence several times with similarly shocking results. From then on, they generally respected the fence and stayed in the pasture.

The animals ate the weeds that grew without cultivation. Vegetables took more work. A few weeks after planting the garden, watering it, and weeding it, Mom thinned the carrots and radishes. Along with pinto beans, potatoes, and Mom's homemade bread for dinner, we had steamed radish greens. And we enjoyed the fresh crispness of tiny golden carrots, red globe radishes, and long white icicle radishes.

With both Dad and Frank getting paychecks, Mom smiled even after she paid the bills. One day she came home with real, store-bought toilet paper.

"Woo-hoo!" Frank exulted.

"Luxury!" Emma added.

"Retire the catalog!" Frank said.

Mom grinned. "Won't hurt to leave it out there in case the real stuff runs out."

Before, we'd taken the softness of toilet paper for granted. Suddenly, it was a luxury to be celebrated.

One morning Dad said, "We've got to get a baler one of these days." He began buying newspapers again and watching ads for farm equipment and auctions. One evening he noticed another kind of ad. "The apricots are ripe up at Ringold Farms," he said. He looked at Mom. "Do we want some?"

Mom smiled. "Do we like fresh fruit?"

"Yeah!" we all chimed.

"And do we want fruit next winter?" Mom added.

"Yeah!" we chorused again.

"But with everyone working so hard, we don't have time to pick like we did the last couple years," Dad added.

"No, we don't," Mom agreed. "But how about U-pick?" She paused. "Now that you and Frank are earning some income, we could buy some. They'll be cheaper if we pick them ourselves. Several of us could go up after you get off work tomorrow afternoon and pick a few boxes just for our use."

The sweet, fresh apricots tasted wonderful! And Mom and I were back at washing jars, washing fruit, filling jars, scalding lids, heating water, timing 25 minutes of boiling, fishing the jars out of the boiling water, and listening for the pop, pop, pop of jars sealing as we prepped more jars full of golden fruit.

Other days, I helped haul and heat water for washing the laundry and plugged in the cord of the electric wringer washer.

"Don't get your hands anywhere near the wringer!" Mom reminded. "It could crush your hand and pull your arm right into it." She ran the soapy, washed clothes through the wringer into the rinse tub filled with water, then ran the rinsed clothes through the wringer again into a dry tub. I'd grown tall enough to reach the clothesline, so I hung much of the laundry. It dried quickly in the desert's dry heat.

Hot day followed hot day. Mama Kitty and her rambunctious brood entertained Hazel—or did she entertain them? She pulled a stick in the sand or taunted them with a moving string. Mama Kitty sometimes wandered away. When she returned with a mouse or a gopher, sticks and strings lost their attraction. The growing balls of fur became ferocious little lions.

Other times I did my best to entertain Hazel by pointing out a horned toad zipping across the sand. (As long as they kept eating insects, they were definitely friends.) We played ball, we invented games, and I pushed the T and wheel. Though we no longer had pavement to roll the wheel on, sand worked fairly well. Besides, the bumps in the sand just gave me a little more challenge. I stood the wheel up for Hazel to try to push. It didn't stay upright very long. I tried to help her, but with two sets of arms often pushing and pulling two different directions, the duo wasn't very successful.

Mama Kitty rubbed against our legs. She let us dress her, and both she and Hazel would listen to my stories and school lessons . . . for a while . . . while playful kittens boxed and wrestled at our feet.

Midday, I suggested Hazel watch for the mailman to come down our road. If we heard a vehicle, it was most likely him—we were the only occupants along our mile-long road. After he came, Hazel held my hand as we walked to the mailbox.

Day followed day. Uncle Max dropped by on occasion to talk farming . . . and he'd tease one or more of us. Sometimes we visited his family at our old shop house. It was fun to have family nearby.

Our growing garden brought delight and dismay. I helped hoe and weed the garden. Helped pick lettuce, zucchini squash, green beans, cucumbers, tomatoes. Mom had figured out better what grew well in the desert heat and what didn't—it was too hot to grow peas unless we planted very early, and we didn't move onto our farm that summer until too late. I missed the sweet crispness of peas fresh from the garden. I wished she hadn't learned that zucchini produced like gangbusters.

Hazel and I sat in the sand and snapped green beans into a large dishpan. Most of the fresh vegetables were a wonderful diversion from the previous winter's pinto beans, potatoes, and carrots! Personally, though, I could have done without zucchini.

One evening at supper, I tried passing the zucchini on without spooning any onto my plate. "Would you like me to help you with the squash?" Dad asked.

I knew better than that. We were expected to take a little of every kind of food on the table. If we took even a tiny amount, all was fine. If we didn't take any, Mom or Dad would serve us.

I swallowed hard, remembering. I had tried skipping oatmeal one time. Only once! I didn't take any—Dad gave me a heaping bowlful. Eventually, I left the table with very little of the *big* bowlful eaten. Lo and behold, at dinnertime, while everyone else ate one of my favorite foods, a bowl of cold oatmeal sat at my place. After chilling in the refrigerator all morning, it had turned into a cold, lumpy, even more distasteful mass. I didn't like *hot* oatmeal. Cold oatmeal? Disgusting!

The cold oatmeal in my bowl didn't disappear very quickly. "Do you like your oatmeal so much you want it for supper too?" Dad asked.

I didn't answer. I didn't even look at him. I swallowed hard— better I keep what I was thinking to myself.

He chuckled. "We don't waste food, you know."

I was well aware of that fact! Slowly, o-o-oh, so-o-o slowly, I choked down the cold oatmeal. By the time I finished, all the other leftovers were in the refrigerator to be used for another meal.

The memory was enough to make me pull the serving bowl of zucchini back from Emma and spoon a small helping onto my plate. Mom caught my eye, smiled, and winked.

As for oatmeal, I much preferred it in cookies. Zucchini? I hadn't thought of a good use for it yet.

CHAPTER 28

Tractor Training

Occasionally, the wind blew, but not as hard as it had at Max's place the year before. Practically before we knew it, the alfalfa stood nearly two feet tall. Purple blooms like tiny pea blossoms began to appear. I stood by the field and breathed in the sweet fragrance.

Dad, Emma, and Frank moved the second sprinkler line from the alfalfa field to the wheat field. The next afternoon Dad hooked the mower onto the power-take-off (PTO) at the back of the tractor. The straight sickle stuck out eight feet on the right side of the rear of the tractor. Dad drove to the field, lowered the mower onto the ground, and turned on the PTO. As he drove, the sharp sickle blades slid back and forth. Tall alfalfa plants fell behind the mower, leaving a flat swath. Dad mowed around the field several times, then Frank mowed until the fragrant alfalfa lay flat, drying in the sun.

A few evenings later, Dad mentioned, "I need to be up by three o'clock in the morning to rake."

"Three?" I asked. "Why so early?"

"That's when the dew's on," Dad answered. "If the alfalfa's too dry when we rake it, the leaves will shatter and fall off. They're the most nutritious part. If they all fall off, nobody will want to buy our hay."

"So why don't we rake it before it gets that dry?"

"If there's too *much* moisture when we rake, it will take too long to dry in the windrows," Dad explained. "If it's too damp when it's baled, it can mold. It can even heat up and start a fire. Farmers have lost whole haystacks because they baled when the hay was too moist."

"But three o'clock?"

"Yep. I better be sleepin' two rows at a time tonight." ("Two rows at a time" was his favorite saying for doing something fast.) He chuckled. "When you're farming, you gotta cooperate with nature. If three o'clock is when the dew is just right, I'll rake . . . or bale . . . at three o'clock. If it's midnight, I'll work at midnight."

When I woke, Dad was on the tractor in the field. The five big metal wheels of the side-delivery rake behind the tractor rolled the mowed hay that had dried flat on the ground into fluffy rows. Most of the alfalfa lay in rows round and around the field.

A couple evenings later, Dad borrowed Glade Farms' baler, and early the next morning I heard a hypnotic clunk, clunk, clunk. The baler swallowed up the rows of loose alfalfa. With each clunk, a plunger packed the hay into firm bales. The machine stretched two wires tight around the length of each bale and knotted them. Then the bales dropped out at the back end of the baler.

But the bales needed to be taken off the field and put in stacks, and we didn't have a hay elevator like Frank and Dale used at Glade Farms. "No problem," Dad said. "We'll build a slip."

"What's a slip?" I asked.

"Well," he said, "it's a piece of equipment that slides along the ground." Pushing his leather hat back, he pulled his red handkerchief out of his back pocket and wiped the sweat off his brow. "But it'd be a lot easier to show you than to explain it. How about if you just watch?"

So Hazel and I watched.

Dad and Frank laid four 2" by 10" boards beside each other with small spaces in between each and a wider space between the two middle boards. Across one end, they bolted a 4 x 4 to the 2 x 10s. They attached a heavy chain near either end of the 4 x 4, then attached the middle of the chain to the tractor's hydraulic lift system and raised the front of the slip barely off the ground.

"Let's try it out," Dad said. He looked up at Frank. "Grab the hay hooks. I'll show you how this thing works."

Frank grabbed the wooden handles of a pair of metal hooks, each about nine inches long. He stood on the side of the slip with a hay hook in each hand. Dad drove slowly, and the slip slipped over the ground. Wasn't hard to figure out where it got its name.

Dad drove the slip beside a bale. "Grab the bale at the back," Dad instructed, "and pull it toward the other side."

Frank hooked the bale. As the slip moved forward, he lifted slightly and swung the bale toward the other side of the slip. The bale slid onto the wood surface. Before long they'd sped up, and Frank could make loading a bale look as easy as eating some of Mom's cookies. He stacked the bales two-high on the slip, then Dad drove near the animal pen. "Hey," he hollered, "would you grab the large pry bar and sledgehammer from over by the shack?"

Frank ran toward the shack, looked around briefly, grabbed the pry bar, then the sledgehammer, and headed back to the slip filled with hay.

"Thanks," Dad said. He jammed the pry bar through the space in the middle at the front of the slip. With the sledgehammer, he pounded the pry bar deeper into the ground. "Stand back," he said, then climbed on the tractor.

Dad put the tractor in low gear and pulled forward a few inches. The bales stayed in place. Slowly, Dad towed the slip out from under them.

"Wow!" Frank said. "Good thinking to leave that space in the middle! What an easy way to unload!"

"It worked slick, didn't it?" Dad said. "We'll stack them later. Let's go get another load of bales now."

They gathered several loads, stacked the bales, then gathered more with the slip. Eventually, the field was bare except for a few broken bales.

"Time for pitchforks," Dad said.

Frank went after a couple pitchforks. Dad noted Emma and me helping Mom with laundry. "Can you spare Helen for a bit?" he asked Mom.

"Sure," she replied. "We can keep an eye on Hazel."

"Good." Dad turned to me. "How about helping us pick up broken bales?"

When Dad, on the tractor, pulled the slip next to a broken bale, Frank pitched hay onto the slip. I tried to help, but as a skinny, small-for-my-age nine-year-old, my efforts were pretty puny. Then we rode to the next bale.

As Frank and I worked, Dad crawled off the tractor.

"Helen," he said, "you're not real good with the pitchfork just yet. I think the job will go faster if you drive the tractor and I help Frank load the hay." Dad reached for my pitchfork. "Ready to learn to drive?"

The thought had crossed my mind. The time had come.

Dad motioned toward the tractor seat. "Climb on up."

From the seat, the steering wheel seemed huge. I stretched and grabbed it with a hand on each side. He showed me the clutch on my left side and the brakes on my right side—one brake pedal for each large, rear tire. He showed me the fuel lever for speeding up or slowing down. He started to show me how to shift, then held up his hand. "Forget shifting for now," he said. He pushed the clutch down with his hand. "Hold the clutch down with your foot."

I put my foot on the clutch. It started to come up, but I moved ahead on the tractor seat and pushed harder.

Dad shoved the gearshift. "Just stay in first gear." He stepped back, away from the tractor.

I let up on the clutch. The tractor lurched forward. I glanced back. Frank swayed on the slip, using his pitchfork to balance. I steered the tractor toward another broken bale. When the slip got close, I pushed on the clutch. It didn't budge.

"Stand on it!" Frank yelled.

With my foot on the clutch, I stood up. The tractor merrily bounced along. I tightened my grip on the steering wheel, pushed my full weight onto the clutch. Nothing happened. Leaning left, I gave a slight jump and plunked all my weight onto the clutch. The pedal sank. The tractor stopped. I heaved a sigh of relief. *It's a good thing the field is flat and I didn't need to step on the brakes at the same time!* I thought.

"Good thing you ate your oatmeal this morning!" Dad laughed. He and Frank carried pitchforks of hay from a little way behind the slip. Since the slip just slid on the ground, reverse wouldn't work. Dad and Frank loaded the loose hay, then Dad called, "Onward, ho!"

The tractor started forward with less of a jolt. Steering got easier and so did starting and stopping. It was kind of fun to drive. For some reason, though, when it was time to drive the load near the fence around the animal pen, Dad drove.

My first experience driving tractor left a lot to be desired. *Will Dad ever trust me to drive again?* I wondered.

CHAPTER 29

Uninvited Guests

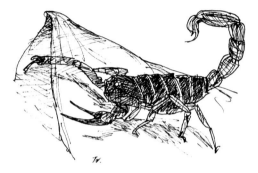

The alfalfa field looked dead. All the green had been mowed, and we hadn't watered that field while the cut hay dried. "It'll be okay," Dad said. "Alfalfa roots grow strong and deep. They've been known to grow more than twenty feet deep."

"Twenty feet?" Emma looked shocked. "That's longer than the shack!"

"You're right," Dad said. "The field will green up when we get water back on it." He turned off water to the two sprinkler lines stretching across the wheat field. Emma drove the tractor, and Dad and Frank loaded the irrigation pipes onto the pipe trailer, then unloaded them in two lines across the alfalfa field again. Sure enough, within days, the field looked green—the alfalfa was growing again.

Whatever else we did, the ram and billy goat kept butting heads— thud, thud, thud . . . Since Frank routinely teased the ram, he kept an eye on his ram whenever he went into the sheep and goat pen.

Mom made lunches for Dad and Frank on the days they went to work at Glade Farms. Morning and evening, Emma or Frank milked the goats and cow. Through the day, Emma changed loads of sprinklers. She or Mom patched or mended clothes that got ripped. Mom taught me how to sew on buttons. Anyone available weeded the garden and picked produce. Mom cooked. I dried dishes and watched Hazel. We all swam in the sump to cool off and bathed in it to get clean—Mom always made sure we had a bar of soap that would float.

One afternoon Dad came home from work at Glade Farms with several sticks about four feet long . . . with a few leaves attached. "Got our first trees!" he announced.

Frank looked sidelong at the leafy stakes sticking out of a dampened burlap bag. "What are you going to do with those?"

"Plant 'em!" Dad said.

"You expect those to grow?"

"Yep. They're poplars," he said. "Lombardy poplars are hardy. These are branches off the Glade Farm trees that Carl said needed to be trimmed. They'll make cheap shade."

Frank laughed. "Not sure there's enough shade for a mouse."

"Give 'em time," Dad said. "If we stick 'em in the ground and water them, they'll grow like gangbusters."

Dad pulled the garden hose slightly beyond the driveway. He planted and watered a row of seven Lombardy poplars. By the next morning their leaves drooped. One or another of us made sure they got frequent watering. It would, after all, be refreshing to have some shade.

Within a few days, the poplar leaves perked up. We kept watering them. Eventually, new leaves formed on Dad's sticks.

The alfalfa field, also, turned green again. The plants grew tall and started to blossom again. Dad hooked the mower to the tractor, and hay harvest started all over. We mowed. The hay dried enough that Dad planned to send Emma out to rake early in the morning. Then rain came. It sounded like music on the metal roof of our granary bedroom. The air smelled fresh and clean.

Unfortunately, the rain threw a monkey wrench into harvest plans. Our hay got wet and had to dry out all over again before we could rake. Dad had already raked Glade Farms' hay into windrows.

It also got wet and had to dry out again. When the hay dried, both farms needed the baler at the same time. It was their baler. We waited.

Dad sold a couple truckloads of bales from the stack of first-cutting hay to a trucker who hauled hay to a dairy in western Washington. He gave the check to Mom. "Take good care of this," he said. "Don't know what this next cutting will be worth—first the rain cut the nutritional value and bleached the color. Then the sun bleached it even more. Dairy farmers want top quality hay." He sighed. "We've got to get our own baler."

He went to more farm auctions, explored prices at equipment dealers, and kept watching ads.

Eventually, the rained-on hay got raked. Then a whirlwind raced through the field. It picked up hay from the neat rows, whirled it around in the air, and scattered it. So, early the next morning, Dad raked again. Within a couple days, the hay was baled and stacked. When it came time to pick up broken bales again, Dad seemed to have forgotten my earlier lack of skills. After lunch, he drafted me to drive again. I did better than before. Enough better that, by third cutting, he drafted me into a new job.

Dad had me ride along as he mowed the first couple rounds of alfalfa. He showed me how to turn a square corner by pressing the right tractor brake, how the mower sickle worked, how to clear a clog out of the sickle guards. "If a narrow row of hay stays standing behind the mower, stop," he said. "Turn the mower off, and check to see if there's hay clogging it or if there's a broken sickle section." He stopped, looked me straight in the eye, and said, "Never get close to the mower with the sickle moving!" He paused. "Never!" he emphasized. "Don't want you cutting off a foot or a hand!"

Dad let that settle in my mind for a moment, then pointed to the small, sharp, triangular blades along the sickle. "If you hit a rock or something, you could break a sickle section. If one breaks, bring the tractor in, and I'll fix it. Any questions?"

"No."

"Think you can handle it?"

My voice wavered. "I thi-ink so."

Dad grinned. "You'll do fine," he said. "I've got to do some repairs on the rake. We'll need it in a few days to rake this hay." He headed to the farmyard.

I started the sickle on its back-and-forth movement, put the tractor in gear, and kept the gas lever on low. I let up the clutch, and the mowing machine was in business. I turned my head constantly, looking forward to see where I was going, backward to be sure the mower was still working and mowing evenly. As I got more comfortable, I sped up a bit.

At the first corner, I turned the gas low. I stood up and pushed all my sixty pounds onto the right brake. The tractor headed off at an angle that wasn't sharp enough to stay by the hay. I stopped the tractor, lifted the mower by raising the hydraulic lever, backed at an angle, lowered the mower, and drove beside the standing hay again. The next corner was a little better, as was the next, and the next, and the next. Soon I was mowing at a reasonable clip and making square corners by pushing all my weight onto the right brake.

Up one side of the field I drove, made a corner, up the next side, made a corner, up another side . . . With each swath, the remaining section of standing hay got smaller. Round and round, I drove. Before long, I started to feel bored. I sang—just loud enough to hear myself over the drone of the tractor engine.

Suddenly, I spotted a telltale row of green behind the mower—while the rest of the alfalfa behind the mower lay flat on the ground, a row a couple inches wide and several feet long still stood tall. I stopped and turned off the mower. I jumped down off the tractor and cleared the hay from the mower. Sure enough, a sickle section was broken. I drove to the farmyard.

Dad saw me coming and got parts and his tools. He replaced the broken section nearly as quickly as I downed a tall glass of water— even warm from the sun on the milk cans, the water felt refreshing. Off I went to mow some more, sing some more, think up poems, and watch to make sure I did a good job.

One afternoon I had a terrible pain in my jaw—a miserable uninvited guest. Whatever we tried, the pain in my mouth kept getting worse.

"We need to take Helen to a dentist," Mom said.

"Can we afford to?" Dad asked.

"That doesn't really matter," Mom answered. "We've tried every remedy I know, and she's hurting terribly."

She called and got an appointment for the next day.

The dentist examined my teeth. "She has several cavities," he said. "I can fill most of them and those teeth won't be any worse for the wear, but one tooth is beyond repair. I'll need to pull it to get rid of the pain."

Mom gave permission.

As the dentist worked in my open mouth, he asked Mom, "Has she been brushing her teeth?"

"Yes," Mom answered, "but we don't have running water, so we all have to brush our teeth outside. In the winter, I imagine we've all hurried too fast."

"That could be the problem. Do you have other children?"

"Yes."

"Why don't you make an appointment on the way out of the office to have them each checked? If they have cavities, let's deal with them before they get to the point where we can't save a tooth."

Mom made appointments. Frank and Emma had cavities too. The whole works of us got lectures on proper teeth brushing, including the importance of *not* rushing . . . even if we were spitting into a snowbank.

One afternoon Frank happened to look out to the northwest. Dad was walking across the pasture, whistling, paying no particular attention to the animals. Suddenly, Frank's eyes got big. Behind Dad, the ram eyed him. The ram lowered his head.

It was too late to yell and get Dad's attention. Frank held his breath. Dad walked on, totally oblivious to the action behind him.

The ram let loose. He raced . . . straight toward Dad. Head down, he hit Dad square in the knees. Dad buckled. He landed on the ram and slid sideways onto the ground.

Frank held his breath as he watched. Dad lay there a minute, then got up. He faced the ram. Frank saw Dad's mouth moving, but could not hear the words. The ram backed off.

Frank headed the other direction—he thought it would be a good time to disappear. He didn't mention what he'd observed. Dad didn't mention it either.

Dad did, however, talk about the animals. "We're going to have a problem this winter," he said, "if we don't make some better arrangements for hauling water."

"Like what?" Mom asked.

"The five- and ten-gallon milk cans work for drinking water, but the irrigation water will be turned off this fall. We'd have to make several trips a day for water for the animals unless we get a good-sized tank for hauling water."

Mom agreed, and Dad started looking for a large tank to put on the truck. Within a couple weeks he purchased a 500-gallon water tank with a frame. The seller loaded it onto our truck and fastened it tight. Come winter, we were ready to haul water.

Along with farm work, we began to make plans for the coming school year. For their junior year, Emma and Frank would go to a boarding high school near Spokane, Washington, about a three-hour drive away. Emma would work in the kitchen and Frank in the dairy to help pay their bills. I continued in elementary school in Pasco.

It seemed strange to have just four of us at home—Dad, Mom, Hazel, and me. Dad looked at my hands. "Hm-m-m. Your hands are a little small for milkin' Bossie." He grinned. "But I betch yer bottom dollar you could milk the goats."

So Dad milked the cow. Sometimes he milked the goats, sometimes I did. After school, I helped drive the tractor some. Thursdays, cleaning the church took longer than when Emma and Frank had helped.

We had no combine to harvest the wheat, so Dad contracted to have it harvested. When I went to school one morning, golden grain waved in the field. When I got home, straw lay in the field. The contractor had hauled most of the wheat to an elevator. Dad raked the straw into windrows. Since straw had no leaves to shatter, he didn't have to wait for the dew. He baled the straw a couple afternoons later. I drove the tractor as Dad loaded the straw bales onto the slip. He even trusted me to drive the tractor next to the straw stack.

A couple weeks later, I overheard Mom say, "The money from the wheat will pay our first year's payment on the land loan."

"That's good news!" Dad said. He chuckled. "We'll get to farm another year."

Mom's quiet voice had a smile in it. "You really do enjoy farming, don't you?"

He smiled. "Yes, I do," he said. He paused, then added, "But I'll be glad when money's not so tight."

"That will be nice," Mom answered. "But for now, we've got money for the land payment before it's due. I think I'll go ahead and pay it right away so we can save a little on the interest."

By late October, nights were getting chilly. Dad and Mom scooted the table and chairs closer to the door. They carried their double bed into the shack and placed it across the east end, opposite the door. Then Dad made a shelf over their bed for a single-bed mattress. We carried it inside and slid it onto the wood shelf. At the back, it barely fit below the cupboards on either side of the window.

"We'll all sleep inside this winter," Mom said. "Hazel can sleep at the back of the top bunk and you, Helen, can sleep by the edge."

That night, I climbed onto our new bed. I crawled over to the window at its side and looked out just to be sure the stars were still there. They were.

Hazel lay down next to the cupboard. She giggled when I squiggled in beside her. The edge of the bed was right beside me. If I fell out of bed, I would splat onto Dad.

A few evenings later, Mom pulled back the covers on their bed. She sat down and started to scoot to her side of the bed, under Hazel's and mine. She turned sideways and started to lie down. "Eeek!" She shot back up. "What's that?"

Shocked by my unflappable Mom's reaction, I jerked my head over the edge of the top bunk and looked down. My breath caught. My eyes got big. There on Mom's pillow sat an uninvited creature that looked like a crawdad, only a lot smaller. A long skinny tail curled up over its back. Two pincers stretched out in front. Though it was small, it looked ferocious.

CHAPTER 30

Christmas Commotion

Dad leaned over the bed, looking toward the ferocious-looking little creature on Mom's pillow. "Ah, hah," he said. "Just a scorpion."

"It startled me," Mom said.

"*Just* a scorpion?" I asked. "It looks scary."

"Probably isn't deadly, but better to avoid his sting." Dad kept his eye on the uninvited guest. "They prefer bugs to people. But it's warmer in here than outside nowadays. He probably just wanted a warmer place to hibernate for the winter."

"Well," Mom exclaimed, "I don't care to share my pillow with him!"

Dad grabbed a piece of paper off the table and leaned toward the scorpion. It raised its pincers and whipped its tail. Dad got a second piece of paper, put one in front of the creature and, with the other, herded it onto the paper. He cupped the paper and took sir scorpion outside.

"He can find a new place to hibernate," Dad said when he returned. "Didn't want to kill him. They eat bugs and spiders we don't really want around."

"Thanks for getting rid of him," Mom said. She picked up her pillow and inspected it, threw back the covers and examined the bed. She smiled. "It's nice he didn't bring any of his relatives with him!"

By late November, the night temperatures dipped into the teens. We looked forward to Emma and Frank coming home for Thanksgiving weekend.

Dad shook his head. "It's too cold to sleep outside," he said. "Even the cellar would be awfully cold. Let me see what I can come up with."

He measured, scratched his head, and pondered. "It'll be cozy," he said, raising an eyebrow, "but, if we scrunch the furniture closer together, Frank's twin bed could fit here." He pointed.

"But will there be room to get between the bed and the counter?" I asked.

Dad pulled out his tape again and showed us how much space would be left. "We can scooch through."

"If we hold our breath," Mom said. She laughed. "It means the world to me for us to be a close family," she added, "but this will take *close* to an extreme I never quite imagined."

Dad brought Frank's single bed frame from the cellar and set it up against the wall, between the table and chests of drawers. Fortunately, the headboard and footboard were the same height. He lay boards over them and added a piece of plywood, then stood back, looking at his creation. "I'll bring Frank's mattress up from the cellar," he said. "Do we have another mattress someplace that we could put on this top bunk?"

"Yes," Mom answered. "We have a twin mattress with the things in storage."

When I got home from school, both beds were made up and ready for occupants.

Mom had made arrangements for Emma and Frank to ride with another student from the same school. When they arrived, Mom met them with big hugs. Then she said, "Come in, come in. Get out of the cold."

Frank stepped to the shack door and stopped abruptly. His eyebrows jutted upward. "Boy, are we going to be cozy this weekend!"

Emma did a quick once-over, plopped her suitcase on the top bed, and declared, "This one's mine." She grinned and glanced at Frank. "Bottom bunk is yours."

Frank looked at the space. His eyebrows arched again. "I'd better breathe before I crawl in. Not sure I can after I get there."

Mom laughed. "You'll be able to breathe," she said, "but you'd better choose a comfortable position from the get-go. Turning over may be a challenge."

When we all turned in that evening, happy banter filled the shack until, one by one, voices silenced and heavy breathing started.

Except for taking care of the animals, as-short-as-possible trips to the outhouse, and brushing teeth, we spent most the days inside. With the body heat of all six of us in the shack, cooking on the stovetop, and baking in the oven, the shack stayed fairly warm. We cooked and ate, had worship, played games, and told stories. What fun for all six of us to be together again!

Sunday came all too fast. We took Frank and Emma back to school.

Back at home in the shack, there was no room for a Christmas tree. Mom gave me several sheets of green construction paper. I cut a Christmas tree shape and crayoned red, yellow, and blue balls onto it. Mom came up with several thumbtacks. I dragged a chair over from the table and tacked the tree against the wall over the chests of drawers.

Dad brought in a bucket of milk and handed it to Mom. He took off his heavy, winter coveralls and hung them on a nail on the inside of the door.

"Since Dad and Frank worked at Glade Farms last summer, can we have Christmas gifts this year?" I asked.

Mom smiled. "Yes, we can."

"When can we go shopping?"

"On December 26." Mom glanced at me. Her eyes twinkled.

"But that's *after* Christmas!"

"But not after *our* Christmas," she said. "Frank is going to stay at school during Christmas vacation," she added. "Somebody has to milk the cows, and the dairy manager has seen Frank is a good worker and can be trusted to do the work well. So Emma will come home, but Frank will stay at school."

"And," Dad jumped in, "that will help pay the school bill. But we'll go see him on December 27."

"Mom's birthday!" I said.

"Yep. And this year we'll celebrate Christmas on her birthday too."

Mom smiled. "We'll all get to be together!" she said. "Can't think of a better birthday present!"

"You gals can cook ahead, and we'll take Christmas dinner with us," Dad added. "As soon as we milk and do the chores that morning, we'll take off. We'll get there after Frank has milked, we'll have the middle of the day together, then we'll leave before he needs to milk the cows in the afternoon."

"Which means," Mom said as she strained the milk into jars, "we can do all our shopping on December 26—when all the after-Christmas sales are on. We'll be able to get nicer things because they'll be less expensive."

Cold day followed cold day. At night, squeezed between the cupboard and me, Hazel poked me with her knee and arm as she turned over in her sleep. The space for me was so narrow that often I slept with one leg hanging over the edge of the bed.

Emma came home a few days before Christmas. On Christmas day we wished each other Merry Christmas and went about everyday chores, listened to Christmas music on the radio, and cooked for our Christmas dinner scheduled for two days later.

The day after Christmas, we donned coats and piled into the pickup. The parking lot at Sears in Pasco was almost full, but Dad found a spot. Though we arrived shortly after the store opened, crowds already filled the aisles. Women surveyed hanging clothing, pawed through shelves of linens, looked at small appliances. Men pondered tools. Children gawked at toys. Shoppers rushed from area to area with armloads of items, then waited in long lines to pay for their treasures.

We joined the commotion.

Clothes that included Christmas figures were marked down a lot. And Christmas wrapping paper was really cheap.

We hadn't had real Christmas wrapping paper for three years, since we'd left our home in the woods. "It's so pretty!" I said. "Can we have some wrapping paper?"

Mom stared at the paper. She looked at the price. I could almost see the cogs turning as she figured the cost in her head. After a long minute, she grinned down at me. "Yes. Which ones would you like?"

Choices. So many choices—red, green, blue, silver, gold. Bells, trees, angels, holly, wise men. I picked out two rolls of pretty wrapping paper. Mom picked up red and green curling ribbon. I didn't know what I was going to wrap, but it was going to be a good Christmas, a pretty Christmas.

At home, we laid Frank's gifts on the table. I wrapped the socks I'd chosen for him with blue paper covered with silver bells. Then I tied red ribbon around it, and Mom showed me how to curl the ribbon with the edge of a scissor blade. With a little practice, I managed more curls. Emma wrapped a shirt.

I sat on the bed looking out the window while Mom and Emma wrapped gifts for me. They just had to look the other way while I wrapped gifts for them and they wrapped gifts for each other. We waited until Dad went outside to do chores to wrap his. Even Mom's birthday gifts were beautiful in their Christmas wrapping paper.

The next morning while Dad milked and fed the animals, we girls packed the gifts and food in boxes, then carried them to the pickup. Shortly, we were on our way. We sang Christmas carols and listened to stories. Dad always had stories. Some we'd heard before, but he told them with such enthusiasm and animation that we asked to hear them again.

By midmorning our family was all together. Just for that day, a simple dormitory room was the best place in the world to celebrate Christmas . . . and Mom's birthday.

CHAPTER 31

Deep Freeze

E arly January weather was mild. Frost covered the out of doors most mornings, but afternoons warmed to above freezing. The temperature got up into the forties several days. But by the thirteenth, the high temp for the day was 30 degrees. Snow started. Days later, the temperature plummeted to zero. Dad crawled out of bed, turned on the oven, and opened the oven door to warm up the inside of the shack. "No wonder it feels cold in here!" He shivered. "There's ice on the water in the wash pan!"

Dad pulled on long johns before he put on his overalls. "If we've got ice in here, I'll sure have to break ice on the livestock's water troughs." He put on his hooded sweatshirt, heavy coveralls, and mittens. "Can't say I'm looking forward to feeding the critters this morning." He opened the door. "Br-r-r-r!" A frosty white puff rose. He pulled the door shut behind him.

He must have hurried. I was still in my nightgown hovering over the oven door trying to get warm when he came back. "Got the animals fed, except for Old Bossie. Gotta warm up before I milk." He joined Hazel and me at the oven. "Good thing I got water in the stock tank just a couple days ago. Don't know if the old truck will start in this kind of weather."

For the next several days the temperature never got above freezing. Snow fell off and on. Mom, Hazel, and I wore our warmest duds when they took me to school. Day after cold day dragged on. The oven pretty much stayed on anytime we were home.

Ten days after the mercury hit zero, it dove to 17 degrees below zero. I was thankful it wasn't a school day. Staying inside entertaining Hazel or having my hands in warm dishwater seemed much preferable to sticking my nose out in the cold.

Dad went outside to do chores. He was gone longer than usual on the really cold mornings. Mom was getting breakfast when he came in. "We've got a problem. We're out of water for the critters, and the truck won't start."

Mom looked up. "What'll we do?"

"I'll think about it over breakfast," Dad said. "Somethin's gotta work."

The weather forecaster on the radio expected the extreme cold to stay with us a while. After breakfast, Dad headed outside again.

Mom left the radio on while I washed dishes and she dried. A commentator talked about unrest in the Southeastern states, about tensions between races. He talked about bus boycotts, about integrating schools, about prejudice.

"What's prejudice?" I asked Mom.

She sighed, squinted her eyes like she was thinking. There was a long pause, then she spoke. "Think about the word," she said. "Prejudice is to pre-judge. To decide about something before you have accurate information."

I frowned, puzzled.

Mom smiled. "Remember the first time you saw Mrs. Morse?"

"Yeah. I didn't like her."

"Why do you think you didn't like her?"

"She scared me."

"She looked different than anyone you'd ever known, didn't she?"

"Yeah."

"After you rode to school with her for a few weeks, what did you think of Mrs. Morse?"

"She's really nice. She's friendly . . . and kind."

"So . . ." Mom responded, "after you had more information, you made a better decision about what she was like. Right?"

"Yeah."

"That's what prejudice is—it's making a decision before you have important information. Sometimes, just because someone is different, people judge them without the information that's necessary to make a good decision."

"Hm-m-m." I stared out the window. "So . . . with Mrs. Morse, I had prejudice at first."

"That's right." Mom paused. "But you learned to make a better decision."

Mom dried dishes and took care of them while I thought about prejudice. "What the news has been talking about," I said, "is people being prejudiced against someone who has a different color of skin."

"Right," Mom agreed.

"So, what's the difference between people?"

Staring out the window, Mom held the dishtowel and oatmeal kettle midair. Then she smiled and turned to face me directly. Remember this last Christmas?"

"Yeah." I smiled.

"Did you enjoy wrapping gifts?"

"Yes. And it was fun to have pretty paper with different colors."

"When you wrapped a gift, did the wrapping paper change the gift?"

"It made the package look different."

"But, did the choice of wrapping paper change the gift that was inside the package?"

"Oh. No. The socks I gave Frank would still have been the same no matter what color of paper I wrapped them with."

"You're right," Mom said. "And it's the same with people. Skin is like wrapping paper. The color of the wrapping paper doesn't change the gift on the inside. A wise person will get to know someone before they pass judgment on them, no matter the color of their skin."

That made sense to me. Blacks and Hispanics were moving into Pasco. When we met someone in town who looked different than we did, Mom smiled. They usually smiled back . . . just like anyone else would. *The world is prettier,* I thought, *with different wrapping paper.*

Late morning, Hazel and I sat on our bed playing with blocks. It hadn't taken long to figure out that heat rises—if the temperature was comfortable below, it was cozy on our top bunk. It was also personal space for Hazel and me—anyone else in the family would have hit their heads on the ceiling, but Hazel and I were short enough to fit.

The shack door opened. A small snowstorm burst in, along with Dad. He closed the door and stepped over by the oven. He pulled off mittens, tossed them on a chair, and reached his hands toward the oven heat. "Well," he said in the midst of shivering, "nothing I've tried has worked. Only one thing left. The tractor's running. I'll hook up a logging chain and tow the truck."

"Tow it?" Mom glanced out the window at the thermometer. "It's four degrees *below* zero out there. You'll sit out in the cold on the tractor and tow the truck for three miles?"

"Not much choice. The animals have to have water."

"You'll freeze!"

"I'll wrap up in every bit of duds I've got."

All was silent except the teakettle hiss as steam rose. Mom turned back to dinner prep. Dad rubbed his hands in front of the oven for a bit. "Helen," he broke the silence, "I'm going to need your help."

I looked over at him from my warm, top-bunk perch.

"I need you to steer the truck."

Mom turned toward Dad. Her eyebrows scrunched closer together. I could almost hear her thinking, *Are you sure?*

Whether or not Mom was okay with the idea, I definitely had reservations. "B-b-but I've never driven the truck," I said.

"I know." Dad sighed. "But you got pretty good at tractor driving last summer. You won't have to worry about anything other than steering."

"Are you sure?" Mom asked. "She's barely eleven . . . and small for her age."

"Are you saying she's a skinny little kid?"

"Well . . . that's about right."

"Yep . . ." Dad's jaw was set. "Good thing she did a bunch of tractor driving last summer." He turned back toward me. "The steering wheel is about the same size as the tractor's. And you can only go as fast as I pull with the tractor. You'll do fine."

"When?" Mom asked.

"How long 'til dinner?" Dad countered.

"Probably twenty minutes. Maybe half an hour."

"Good. That'll give me time to thaw out." He glanced at me again. "Then we can bundle up and go first thing this afternoon."

Right after dinner, Dad hooked up the chain. On the way to the truck, the dry cold whipped my face. I could barely walk for all the winter wraps. Dad opened the truck door and motioned me in. I crawled up onto the seat. He showed me which pedal was the brake. "Don't think you'll need it. I'll go slow." He looked down, then grinned. "Hm-m-m. You'd have to slide under the steering wheel to reach the brake, huh? Don't worry about it. I'll go slow enough that you won't need it."

I tried to turn the steering wheel. "I can't steer it!"

"That's 'cause it's sitting still," Dad said. "Once we start moving, you'll be able to."

I looked up. All I could see was the dashboard. "I can't see!" I wailed.

"Sit up taller!"

I stretched my spine the furthest it had ever been stretched. By looking under the top of the steering wheel, I could see just over the dash and view the top half of the tractor. Dad slammed the door shut. My heart pounded. I took a deep breath. *Can I do it?* I wondered. *I have to!* "Please, God, help me!" I whispered.

Dad climbed onto the tractor and started it. He looked back as the tractor moved forward slowly. The truck jerked. I tightened my grip on the steering wheel. We started to move. At first, we went straight ahead. But at the end of the driveway, we'd have to turn left. As we approached, I pulled for all I was worth on the left side of the steering wheel. We turned. The truck followed the tractor up the snow-covered gravel road. I gave a sigh of relief. In half a mile was another left turn. Again, I gave it all the strength I had and we made the turn. Another sigh.

In a mile was another ninety-degree corner. This time we had to turn right, and I had to turn in plenty of time to stay on the road and miss the row of three mailboxes.

The tractor turned. I pulled for all I was worth with both hands on the right side of the steering wheel. It turned a little. I tried harder. The truck turned very little more. I pulled with everything I could muster. Then harder still.

Dad and the tractor went up the road. The truck headed for the mailboxes.

My heart pounded. I cranked the steering wheel to the left. The truck slid at a 45-degree angle and dropped down cab-first into the ditch. Clunk. Clunk.

I felt relief for an instant—I'd steered between the stop sign and mailboxes, barely missing both. But the truck was still rolling. In a flash, the chain pushed against the mailbox posts. The three mailboxes crashed to the ground.

The truck stopped. There it sat in the ditch.

My heart nearly jumped out of my chest. *Will Dad be mad? I ruined the mailboxes. How are we going to get the truck out of here?* I slouched back onto the seat.

Dad backed up the tractor to give some slack. He unhooked the chain, then walked toward the truck, white puffs rising with every breath.

I felt freezing cold and burning hot all at the same time. Tears brimmed. *What's he gonna say?* I worried. My heart pounded.

CHAPTER 32

A Lot of Chicken Little

Dad walked over to the truck that sat nose-dived into the ditch. He surveyed the situation, then opened the truck door beside me. "I guess this is harder to steer than the tractor," he said in a calm voice, "but we'll get it out of the ditch. You just wait here."

I breathed again.

He tugged the mailboxes closer to the road, backed the tractor into the ditch just ahead of the truck, and hooked up the chain. He opened the truck door again. "Let me turn those wheels," he said.

He stepped up on the running board, reached over me, and pushed and pulled the steering wheel. He looked at the wheels, then came back and turned them a little more. "Okay," he said. "I'll go slow. See up there just a little ways?" He pointed. "Where the ditch isn't as deep?"

"Yeah."

"We'll go straight up the ditch until there, then I'll pull just a little to the right until we're back up on the roadway. You just follow me. Okay?"

"But I knocked down the mailboxes," I wailed. "We've got to fix them."

"Yes, we do. But there's no mail on Sunday, so we'll go ahead and get the water. When we get home, I'll get a shovel and whatever else I need and come back and fix the mailboxes good as new. That won't be hard since you managed to steer between them and the stop sign. You did the best thing you could do, under the circumstances. Good thinkin'." He stepped down onto the ground. "By the way," he added, "when we get to the next corner, I'll go slower."

I swallowed hard. "O-o-o-kay," I stammered. I stretched tall again so I could get a partial view of where we were headed. The tractor started to pull. The truck moved, oh, so slowly. Down the ditch, then slowly up onto the road again. We were in business. At the next corner, Dad did go slower, and I steered as hard as I could muster. We made it to the well house.

"You stay in the truck and keep as warm as you can," Dad said. He turned on the water, filled the five- and ten-gallon cans with water for the house, then put the hose into the 500-gallon tank. Dad climbed into the passenger side of the truck. "May as well stay out of the wind while that's filling."

It took a long time to fill. There may not have been wind in the cab, but with minus four degrees outside and a truck that wouldn't start, I shivered a bunch. Intermittently I made fists inside my gloves, rubbed my arms, and wiggled my feet and legs, trying to keep the blood flowing. Dad got out and checked on the water once in a while. "Don't want to run it over and make ice here for everyone to slide on."

Finally, the tank filled. Dad turned off the water and tightened the lid on the tank. "Ready to head home?"

"I'm so frozen I don't know if I can move my arms." I wiggled some more, trying to limber up.

As Dad started the tractor, my heart pounded. My anxiety eased some on the straightaways but grew as we approached each corner. We made them all—whew!

Dad towed the truck to just across the fence from the watering troughs. Both Dad and I hurried inside, peeled off layers, and stood on either side of the oven door until we no longer felt like ice cubes.

Eventually, Dad started pulling on his warm clothes again. "Got an errand to run," he told Mom. "A little repair to some mailboxes." He glanced at me and grinned.

Three weeks later—just a few days into February, the cold broke and the temperature climbed into the forties again, then fifties. Dad started talking about crops. Mom started looking at garden seed catalogues. "I've been thinking," Dad said over supper one evening, "it would be good to have something extra to supplement the farm income. How about some chickens?"

"A few chickens for fresh eggs would be nice," Mom answered.

"I was thinking of something more," Dad said. "Of selling eggs. Of getting . . . maybe . . . five hundred chicks."

Mom's eyes got big. "And where are you going to put five hundred chickens?"

"We have some straw bales from last year's wheat," he said. "We can build walls out of straw bales. That'll be warm in the winter and cool in summer. And we can put a roof on it and fence in an outdoor yard too."

"You've already given this some thought, haven't you?"

Dad grinned. "Yep. For laying hens we'll want white leghorns. The bigger chickens are used more for meat, and they don't lay as many eggs. The leghorns eat less and lay more. Seems like a good mix to me."

"And where are you going to get five hundred chicks?" Mom asked.

"The cheapest place to get them is a hatchery that mails them."

Dad and Mom went on discussing what we'd need. Within a few days, Dad was building a chicken coop out of straw bales. It would be about twice as wide and twice as long as our people house. A solid wood door would be on the end closest to the shack.

One morning before I left for school, the phone rang. Dad answered. "Hello . . . Yes . . . Yes, we can come this morning . . . Okay . . . Thank you."

"What was that about?" Mom asked.

"The post office. They want us to hurry up and come get the noisy boxes of baby chicks!"

When I got home from school that afternoon, I'd barely gotten out of the car when I heard cheep, cheep, cheep, cheep, cheep. The chicks made quite a din. "No wonder the post office wanted to get rid of these!" I exclaimed.

"Yep," Dad answered. "There in that stone-walled building, five hundred chicks made an awful racket!" He chuckled. "Want to see the little noisemakers?"

We went into the chicken coop. A sea of tiny yellow fluff balls greeted me. "Looks like you'll have some new chores," Dad said.

And so it was. Feeding and watering chicks, checking the temperature in the chicken house, and turning the heat lamps off and on, depending on the temperature, soon became a part of my assignments on the farm. Within days, tiny white wing feathers began to appear among their downy, yellow coats. As weeks went by, more white feathers grew and replaced the soft, fluffy down. The chicks grew rapidly. Soon their legs seemed too long for the size of their bodies. Before many weeks passed, their bodies caught up and they began to grow tiny red combs on top of their heads.

"They're changing from chicks to pullets," Dad said.

My brow furrowed. "Pull it?" I asked.

Dad chuckled. "Not pull it," he said. "Pullet—spelled p-u-l-l-e-t. When they're bigger than chicks, but haven't started laying eggs yet, they're called pullets."

Days passed. The tiny peeps coming from the chicken house disappeared, and the fowl began making a happy purring, growling sound as we fed and watered them day after day.

As the chickens grew, the radio news was full of talk of Celilo Falls and The Dalles dam. In school, we wrote reports on both. The Dalles dam was a huge, five-year project. It would provide hydroelectric power and improve taking boats and barges up the Columbia River to inland ports. Improved shipping would lower the cost of transporting products. It also would help protect those who lived downriver from seasonal, destructive flooding.

Celilo Falls, on the other hand, was a natural wonder. On its banks had been the oldest continuously inhabited community in North America and a gathering place for Native Americans for thousands of years. Tribes from far and near had come to fish, trade, and socialize. Lewis and Clark on their trip west to the Pacific Ocean portaged around it. Amazed by the falls' power and beauty, they referred to it as "the Great Falls." The rugged rocks and cliffs crossing the river created a stark beauty. The roar of Celilo Falls was unforgettable. It was one of the top six waterfalls by volume in the world, even greater than Niagara Falls.

March 10, 1957 was a happy and a sad day—happy for those who had worked hard for the advancement of hydroelectric power and transportation; happy for those who had worked hard building The Dalles dam. But it was a sad day for the residents of the villages that would be submerged, sad for people who had provided for their families and their tribes by fishing at Celilo Falls for generations, sad for many who had heard the roar and pondered the power and the grandeur of the magnificent waterfall.

About ten thousand people stood above the rising water behind the dam . . . watching—watching a way of life disappear. By the end of that day, Celilo was a memory never to be forgotten by those of us who had seen it and heard it.

At school, as we talked about what was happening, one of my classmates said, "One thing I like is that they are going to build campgrounds by the lake behind the dam."

"Does your family go camping often?" the teacher asked.

"Oh, yes. We go camping every chance we can in the summer." He went on talking about picnicking, swimming, carrying water, using an outhouse, hiking, looking up at the stars at night.

I rolled my eyes. I didn't get it. Why would anyone *choose* to go where you had to carry water? Where you had to use an outhouse?

As for swimming, I could go swimming every day all summer in our sump. Hiking? I did enough hiking just helping with sprinklers, feeding creatures, keeping Hazel away from the canal. Stars? I'd looked up at them many a night. They didn't change much from night to night. It wasn't bad in the summer, but, frankly, when it was 17 degrees outside, I buried my head under mounds of covers and let the stars take care of themselves.

If my classmate and his family wanted to go camping, fine. But I was looking forward to the day when we could *quit* camping. When we could have a house big enough to wiggle in. When we could have the piano and I could play it every day. When we could brush our teeth in a warm bathroom. When we could be finished with the outhouse. When would that day come?

CHAPTER 33

Eggs and Space

S pring continued to warm. Dad built a chicken-wire fence around a pen next to the chicken house. The tiny openings in the fence were small enough that a chicken couldn't get out and most predators or creatures that would want to steal the chickens or their food couldn't get in. He made a small hole in the straw wall and covered it with a door that could slide up and down. In the evenings, when the chickens heard us adding feed inside their house, they scurried in and we closed the door behind them—further protection from nighttime predators.

Dad built nesting boxes in the chicken house. About the time school let out and the other farm work increased, he came in with the first egg. There seemed to be a few more every day. The chicken sounds changed to clucking and cackling.

Leaves developed on the poplar trees. "Someday!" Dad said. "Someday we'll have some shade."

Frank and Emma returned home from school. Hot weather hit. The shack was too hot and too crowded. We moved beds again. Frank slept in the cellar, we girls in the granary, and Mom and Dad under the stars beside the shack.

The hens began laying more and more eggs. Mom began cooking more eggs than we'd ever had before. The yolks of the fresh eggs were a bright orange. They had a deeper, richer flavor than eggs Mom had occasionally bought. She scrambled eggs, fried eggs, boiled eggs, poached eggs, used eggs in casseroles, included eggs in salads. Frank and Dad enjoyed egg salad sandwiches in their lunches when they worked at Glade Farms.

Soon egg-gathering became quite a production—100 eggs, 150, 400. We sold eggs. Preparing them for selling took processes and equipment new to me.

First, we sanded the eggs. Washing them would remove a protective layer, so we used a hand sander to clean off dirt, flecks of manure, and various other things nobody would like to look at when they opened a box of eggs they bought at the grocery store.

I became the main sander of eggs—my first paying job. I received a nickel for sanding a tray of thirty eggs. It definitely was not a get-rich-quick scheme!

Once they were sanded, Mom candled the eggs. The candler looked like a round, metal, gallon can. It could lie on its side (held steady by four little feet) or stand on one end. The other end had a round hole with rubber padding around it. When Mom plugged the candler into electricity, a light bulb inside shone. One by one, she held an egg against the hole. If a dark spot showed, there was a blood clot inside. Mom set those eggs aside for our own use. (When she later broke those eggs, she would separate the blood clot and throw it away.)

After candling the eggs, Mom weighed each one on an egg scale. It showed the exact weight. She had marked on the scale the different sizes—small, medium, large, extra-large, and jumbo. After she weighed an egg, she set it in a tray with others of the same general size. Each tray held thirty eggs.

She placed ten trays of eggs in a box. Dad or Mom took them to a grocery store in town that happily purchased all the fresh eggs we could supply. Some days they took one box of three hundred eggs, some days two boxes.

Life fell into a routine. Water the animals, feed the sheep and goats, milk the cow, feed and water the chickens, listen to the morning news and weather forecast, eat breakfast, have worship, let the chickens out of their house into their pen, gather eggs, change sprinklers, weed the garden, eat lunch, listen to Paul Harvey News on the radio, clean eggs, weigh eggs, box them. The chickens panted when the weather got hot. They drank more water than on cooler days. We needed to check the water and replenish it frequently for all the animals. Shear sheep, sell wool. Mow hay, rake hay, bale hay, stack hay, bring in broken bales, change the sprinklers again . . . and again. Each day was a merry-go-round of activity.

Often while I sanded eggs and Mom kneaded a pan full of bread dough, Hazel would plead, "Tell me a story."

Mom often responded, "What story do you want?"

Hazel had a few favorites. Sometimes she'd say, "You choose."

And Mom would start a story. Her voice carried excitement, curiosity, amazement, sadness, delight—whatever she told, her expressions made the story come to life. Sometimes we cried, more often we laughed.

Thursdays we cleaned the church. Weekends we attended church and sometimes went to a church picnic—Mom's fresh-baked bread, her potato salad, her deviled eggs, or whatever else she took was always popular. If there was a softball game after the picnic, Dad and Frank were in the middle of it.

Occasionally we had a surprise and a break from routine. One morning when I got up, I heard Mom and someone else laughing. The laughter sounded vaguely familiar. I walked out of the granary. A car sat in the driveway—a Hudson. My heart skipped a beat. Only one family I knew drove a Hudson.

I walked around the corner. Mom and Aunt Verda talked and laughed. Blankets with kids wrapped in them were sprawled across the weeds that would someday be a yard.

"And don't worry about food," I heard Aunt Verda say. "We brought enough to feed your family, our family, and an army besides."

We cousins romped and laughed the day away. We waded in the canal, watched water skippers skittle over the water's surface, played kickball. We urged Dad to walk on his hands, and he entertained us with his upside-down antics. And Mom and Verda, not just sisters-in-law, but dear friends from way back, talked and laughed, picked garden produce, and served a picnic feast.

That night we cousins slept on the haystack. The next day we played more, ate more, and laughed more. But before the day was over, they climbed back into their Hudson, and dust billowed up behind them as we waved from our sandy weed patch, and they waved out the windows of their car until we could no longer see each other.

"That was fun!" Mom exclaimed.

"Yep," Dad said. "But now, we'd better get back to work."

Dad continued shopping for a baler and finally came home from a farm auction with one that needed repairs. Fortunately, he was creative and mechanical. Soon, we no longer had to depend on the generosity of Dad's employer to bale our hay. Because we could bale at the prime time, the hay quality also improved. And so did the payment we received.

In town, as Pasco grew west, many considered the old gravel pit to be an eyesore. Edgar Brown, the owner, sold it to the school district for $25,000.00 with the stipulation that the huge hole be used for a stadium. Work began in earnest. Pasco High School students eagerly anticipated having their own stadium.

On a wider scale, day after day, the national radio news talked more and more about a space race. The United States and the USSR (Union of Socialist Soviet Republics) both wanted to prove they had the most advanced technology. They each worked to launch the first satellite into space to orbit the earth. Who would be first?

1957–1958

CHAPTER 34

The Race is On

While the two countries sparred and the newscasters debated, I had my own conundrum—after my winter escapade with steering the truck, would Dad ever let me drive again? I need not have worried. I was simply part of the crew. Mowing hay became a job with my name on it.

One thing I enjoyed while mowing was listening and watching for wildlife. I loved the birdsong I could hear above the purr of our small tractor's engine. Admired the color and crow of pheasants. Delighted in the clear, flute-like meadowlark melody. Treasured the instants when I spotted a cottontail rabbit running away from the hum of the tractor and the clatter of the mower.

If there wasn't any wildlife to note, I could always sing. Or was my singing the reason there wasn't any wildlife? Or I could create poetry . . . or figure out faster ways to gather the eggs and sand them.

At first, the hens laid a few small eggs, lots of medium size, and occasional large ones. By August, as the hens matured, they hardly ever laid a small egg, only a few medium, lots of large and extra-large, and quite a few jumbo eggs. That was great, because the larger the eggs, the more we got paid for them. The size of the egg didn't make any difference with my pay, however—it was still five cents for hand-sanding thirty eggs.

Out of every dime I earned, I set aside one penny for tithe that I took to church. Once when I went to the grocery store with Mom, I bought a candy bar for myself. It tasted sweet and good, but, within minutes, it was gone, and I had nothing to show for my work. *If I'd save my money,* I thought, *I'd have a head start for Christmas gifts.* So, when Mom paid me for my work, I dropped the pennies, nickel, dime, or sometimes a quarter, into a small box in the back corner of my clothes drawer and put the appropriate number of pennies for church in a separate box.

As the school year approached, the radio news talked more and more about the space race. Frank and Emma went back to boarding school for their senior year. We moved Mom and Dad's full-size bed and Hazel's and my single bed back into the shack.

I started sixth grade. That year I walked half a mile to a country intersection, rode to town with a neighbor who worked in Pasco, then walked another mile and a half to school. When school was dismissed, I reversed the process, doing homework in her unlocked car while I waited until she got off work.

Friday, September 13, was a greatly anticipated day for Pasco High School sports fans. The football game would be against rival Walla Walla. Could Pasco win in the first game in their own new Edgar Brown Stadium?

Or would they even get to play in the new stadium? Workers were still working . . . until an hour and a half before the game. Even though only half the lights were working, they still had more light than at the old field. They celebrated soundly when Pasco pulled off a 16–14 victory!

Less than a month later, October 4 went down in history. USSR launched Sputnik, the first satellite. The newscasters talked on and on about the USSR. How far superior was their technology to ours? Were they a threat to the United States?

The satellites grabbed our attention, and that of many others. KALE radio built a tiny studio above their transmitter at Court

Street and Road 68 west of Pasco—at that time, it was far enough out in the country to have very little light pollution. When announcements came about another satellite about to be launched, one of the station's announcers would broadcast from the temporary studio.

Just a month after their first launch, November 3, the USSR launched a second satellite. This one had a dog as a passenger.

We turned on the radio at the expected time of its appearance over our area. At the studio, the announcer talked as he watched for the satellite. As soon as he announced that he spotted it, we donned coats over our pajamas, turned the sound up loud, and went outside, leaving the door ajar so we could hear the radio. We stared at the sky, listening to the announcer tell where to look, what direction the satellite was headed, what star constellation it was near, etc.

"There it is!" Mom exclaimed, pointing it out for the rest of us.

Shivering, we watched in wonder as the manmade satellite sprinted across the sky.

As soon as it disappeared, we headed for the shack, turned off the radio, warmed up by the oven door, and crawled into bed.

Mom cooked up a storm when Emma and Frank came home for Thanksgiving weekend. We had such fun when we were all together. But, after the weekend, they went back to school.

The United States scheduled a satellite launch for December 6. We listened to the radio in suspense. When would it be visible in our area?

It wouldn't. It exploded on the launch pad. The news was full of sadness at the failure.

As Christmas approached, I pulled the box of money out of my drawer and counted it. I had saved enough to get small gifts for each member of my family. I thought and planned. I shopped with delight. The Woolworth clerk was patient as we counted out my change. That Christmas was special for me—I had saved, planned, and served my family from my own work.

The United States finally launched a satellite successfully on January 31, 1958. On February 3, the USSR's attempt to launch Sputnik 3 failed. And so it went . . . back and forth . . . USSR and USA . . . successes and failures. But whenever possible, we were out at night marveling at mankind's ingenuity to have equipment high above us, circling the earth.

Over meals, we wondered aloud where the space race would lead humanity. We talked about it at school. But we always got back to real life—math, hauling water, sanding eggs, and reading.

Dad continued reading aloud to the family. He read books. He read magazines. We all enjoyed the articles from *Reader's Digest*. We especially enjoyed "Life in These United States," "Humor in Uniform," and any of the short humor. Whether we listened while preparing a meal, cleaning up afterwards, or dealing with eggs, laughter filled the shack.

One clear winter afternoon Dad sat at the table and read aloud as I sanded eggs and Mom candled and weighed them. Hazel and I both sat cross-legged on the top bunk. "Look!" Hazel exclaimed. "What a pretty dog!"

I glanced out the window where she pointed.

Dad dropped his book, jumped up, turned around, and leaned close to us to look out the window.

The golden-colored dog trotted down the gravel road, seemingly oblivious to anything around him. I'd never seen a dog around our farm.

"That's not a dog!" Dad exclaimed. "It's a coyote! And we have chickens!"

1958

CHAPTER 35

Crew Shrinks, Work Doesn't

A *coyote?* I wondered. The golden dog trotting down the road just looked like a friendly dog. I'd heard plenty of coyote yips and howls off in the distance. I'd learned to enjoy hearing them. But I'd never before seen one.

Dad whirled around. In a couple steps, he was by the door. He reached behind the chests of drawers. When he pulled his arm out, he held his shotgun.

"Don't hurt it!" I cried.

Mom looked out the window in front of the counter where she was candling eggs.

Dad slid out the top drawer in a flash. He reached in. Pulled out a handful of shotgun shells. Raced out the door.

My heart pounded. I watched out the window, wanting to see, but, at the same time, not wanting to.

Bang!

The coyote turned its head our direction and trotted faster.

Bang! A second gunshot.

The coyote took off. A puff of dust rose behind him. He ran down the road, headed away from our place.

Bang! A third shot. The coyote raced even faster, not slowing until it was out of sight.

Dad came back in. "I didn't hurt it," he said, "but I needed to scare it."

He made sure no shells were in the gun, put the gun back in its place, and dropped the leftover shells back into the drawer. "Don't want him getting comfortable around here," Dad said. "It was a healthy-looking coyote, so he's getting food someplace. Don't want him to find our chickens!"

"Oh my, no!" Mom blurted.

"A coyote can make short work of a flock!" Dad added. "Of course, the chickens would make such a ruckus that we'd probably hear them if we were home. So, we might only lose a few the first time, but . . ." he paused, ". . . if a coyote found them, he'd be back for more!"

"Thank God he didn't find them!" Mom said.

"Yep. The chickens are providing our bread and butter this winter."

"Not too much bread and butter," Mom said. "Not after we pay the bill for the food to keep them alive, the heat to keep them warm, and the extra hours of light to keep them laying eggs."

"True. But at least it helps. Especially since we haven't been able to sell much hay. Stacks of hay and no buyers." Dad sighed. "And Glade Farms doesn't have much work for me in winter." He walked back to the table, sat in his chair, and picked up his book again. But he didn't open it. He just sat there, staring into space.

Mom lifted another egg, held it to the candler, weighed it, and set it in the "extra-large" tray. She looked up at me. "Do you have any more ready?"

"Yeah. Just a couple more eggs to sand before this tray's full." I set the egg I'd just finished sanding in the tray and cleaned one more. "Tray's ready." I carefully set it in Mom's upstretched hands.

Dad laid his book back down on the table. He took a deep breath. "I've been thinking . . ." he started.

Mom rolled her eyes. "Oh, oh." She grinned.

Dad snickered. All was quiet for a moment, then he said, "We've sold several truckloads of hay, but we have quite a stack we haven't been able to sell. Our animals use the broken bales, but they haven't used up the hay that got rained on. That's the hay that's hard to sell."

"Yes?" Mom asked. "And what do you propose?"

"Well . . ." Dad cleared his throat. "If we raised some cattle, they could eat any hay that doesn't sell. Besides," he continued, "having cattle, would be like having money in the bank. We can't necessarily sell a load of hay anytime we need money, but there's a cattle auction every week. We could take a steer to the auction any time we need to. Or take several."

Mom candled a few more eggs. "And . . . where do you propose to get them?"

Dad lifted his arm and pointed west. "The new dairy down the road apiece keeps their heifer calves, but they're looking for someone to buy their bull calves."

"Calves?" Mom asked. "How old?"

"Days."

"So, they'd need to be bottle fed?"

"Yep, for a while."

"And . . . who around here doesn't have enough to do?"

"Well . . . no one's bored." Dad took some deep breaths. "But we're not getting as many eggs as we did when the hens were in their prime. They're apt to keep going downhill. I'm thinking cattle might be less work and give us more income."

After several discussions over the next couple weeks, Dad purchased calf bottles, nipples, and milk replacer. "Bossie won't give enough milk for us and all the calves," Dad said.

He built a small barn. A few days later when I arrived home from school, four calves had joined our menagerie. Bottle-feeding calves was a new job to fit in between feeding and watering the other critters. The eggs still needed to be gathered, sanded, candled, weighed, boxed, and sold. We huddled around the open oven door when it was cold outside. We all still wanted three meals a day. And we watched satellites at night!

I got to take a vacation from the routine over one night—I stayed with a friend in town. Ah-h-h—no chores, the room was warm all night, and there was running water and a flush toilet indoors. I also had half a regular size bed to myself—no little knees or elbows poking me at intervals all night long. When I arrived home the next day, Hazel snapped, "You need to stay home."

"Why?" I asked.

"I fell out of bed."

Dad chuckled. "Made for a rude awakening. I was sleeping like a log . . . and kerflop . . . she landed in the middle of me."

I looked Hazel in the eye. "You had the whole bed."

"But you weren't there to keep me from falling."

"So, I have another job—be a wall to protect my sister from falling out of bed and Dad from rude awakenings."

"Yeah!" Hazel said.

"Sounds good to me," Dad added with a grin.

Winter finally melted into spring. The alfalfa field turned from tan to green. A bachelor moved in at the end of our road and started to work the land that cornered ours. We always waved when he drove by, usually headed to town in late afternoon. Otherwise, we didn't see him often, but I sometimes heard his dog bark.

As if four calves weren't enough, another one or three increased our small herd every few days. The cute little black and white Holstein calves bounced and frolicked. Whichever one of us humans entered the barn with bottles full of milk won the popularity contest of the hour.

Lambs and kid goats were born. Did Dad decide the income from the calves would be more than that from lambs and wool? Was he just tired from too much work? Did we need the money? Or did he hold a grudge against the ram?

I don't know. But one day when I came home from school, the sheep were gone. "Sold 'em," Dad said.

With spring, Dad changed sprinklers. We moved beds again—Dad and Mom's sat outside on the north side of the shack where they could look at the night sky, Hazel and I moved back into the granary. The alfalfa grew. School ended. Frank and Emma graduated. They both took jobs elsewhere and moved away. The crew shrank. But the work didn't.

The morning Emma left, Dad looked at me. "Well, kiddo," he said, "looks like it's just you and me in the fields nowadays."

Dad fed and watered the large animals and milked the cow. Whoever could, fed the calves. Mom took over more responsibility for the chickens. I tried changing sprinklers. I was eleven, but about as big around as a broomstick. I couldn't lift, balance, and carry a forty-foot pipe on my own. At four and a half years old, Hazel took the job I'd done for Emma when we first moved onto our own farm—she carried the light end of a sprinkler pipe.

When our alfalfa grew, so did Glade Farms' alfalfa. Before Dad went off to mow the hay at Glade Farms one morning, he mowed a couple rounds around one of our fields. He left the tractor in the field near the house and walked in. He pushed his leather hat back and wiped the sweat off his forehead. Looking at me, he said, "It's all yours, kiddo. I've got to go to work. I filled the gas tank, checked the oil, and checked the mower to be sure it was in good shape. It should work fine, but if you have any trouble, just turn off the tractor, leave it where it is, and walk in. I'll check it out when I get home."

CHAPTER 36

Why Did I Ever Want to Drive?

I t was a good thing I'd started driving the tractor before!

Mowing wasn't bad except for one thing—every now and again a pheasant hen would fly up just as the mower passed by. Then I began noticing that when one flew up, part of the time, her feet were missing—the mower had cut off her legs. *Why would she wait so long to escape?* I wondered.

The next time a pheasant flew up as the mower passed, I stopped the tractor and looked behind the mower. In a small depression amidst the alfalfa was a nest full of eggs, some whole, some broken. I recoiled. My stomach tightened into knots. I felt like losing my breakfast. A pheasant couldn't likely survive without feet. A mother had given up her life trying to protect her young.

But it got worse. Sometimes when a hen flew up, her eggs had already hatched. I looked at downy chicks the mower had cut to pieces. A whole family of pheasants decimated. I knew I had to go on. I crawled back on the tractor and cried as I mowed.

208

Dinner gave a welcome break from my sadness, even though I wasn't very hungry. By the time I needed to go back to mowing, the sun beat down, unmercifully hot. What could I do to keep cooler? The straw hat I'd started wearing shaded my face from the direct sun. It helped some, but not nearly enough. I puzzled for a minute, then got an idea. I set my straw hat upside-down on the counter. I grabbed my washcloth off its hook, opened it flat, and lay it in the hat. I pulled an ice cube tray out of the freezer compartment in the refrigerator, emptied several cubes onto the washcloth, and put my hat on, careful to keep the ice cubes on top of my head.

Through the first couple hours, moisture dripped slowly down front, back, or sides of my head. It helped enough that I often repeated the unusual cooling contraption on especially hot afternoons.

I had found something that helped cool me on hot days. Unfortunately, I didn't find a way to keep pheasants from nesting in alfalfa.

A few evenings later, at the supper table Dad looked at me and said, "Now that you're tractor driver number one around here, I may wake you up at three or four in the morning . . . if the dew is right."

Ugh! In years past, sometimes I'd wakened to hear the tractor droning as someone else raked hay. I'd heard the baler's thud, thud, thud as its plunger packed hay tight into bales. But, glad that I could, I went back to sleep. Since Emma and Frank were gone, I knew my "early morning" time was coming, but I definitely wasn't ready for it! I drew in a deep breath.

"I'll check it first thing," Dad said. "If it's not right for raking, I'll let you sleep."

I knew we needed to get the hay raked, baled, and stacked so we could get water back on the field, but it was awfully tempting to wish the dew wouldn't be right until after breakfast. *Hm-m-m. Why did I ever want to drive?*

Sometimes I raked by tractor light and moonlight at 3:00 a.m. On those mornings I often looked to the sky to see if I could spot a satellite going over. Some mornings I began at four o'clock when it was just barely getting light.

After several early mornings it was hard to stay awake as the tractor droned. I started singing to keep myself awake—not loud, mind you. I didn't want to bother anyone who had the luxury of sleeping during normal hours. Just loud enough to hear myself over the engine of the tractor and the swishing of the rake wheels rolling hay into windrows.

Round and round the field. I watched as darkness slipped silently away, as color tinted the eastern sky. I marveled as pink, purple, orange, red danced together and faded into each other. I glimpsed the first curve of golden sun peek above the horizon, find it safe to rise, and burst up in brilliance to wake the world.

Above the hum of the tractor, I heard pheasants crow and meadowlarks flute their shrill, marvelous melody.

The color extravaganza reminded me of the blue and purple flower I'd seen up at Max's place. "There's beauty everywhere," I spoke aloud. "Some places you just have to look a lot harder." The tractor's steady engine sound lulled my mind. I smiled as I looked around. *As much I loved our home in the woods*, I realized, *there truly is beauty in the wide-open spaces too. And . . .* I was surprised by my own thought. *And this is feeling like home.*

Occasionally I got an extra dose of raking. Whirlwinds that marched across the landscape like tiny tornadoes ordinarily didn't do much damage. But when a whirlwind flew through a field where the alfalfa lay in neatly raked rows, it scattered the hay in its path hither and yon. Chasing down the errant hay with the baler was impractical, so I raked it back into rows the baler could efficiently handle.

Sometimes when I raked early, I saw our new neighbor weave his way down our road on his way home. He frequented bars and apparently rarely left them until they closed at 2:00 a.m. He generally arrived home between 2:30 and 3:30 a.m., sometimes later.

Our family's bedtime was significantly earlier—especially during haying. One night when Dad planned to check the moisture of the mowed hay early the next morning and Mom and I were cleaning up in the kitchen, Dad yelled, "Come here! Quick!"

We ran outside, over by the bed where Dad lay.

"Look!" he said, arm lifted skyward. "That looks like a satellite!"

Mom spotted it. "Yes, it does. But we didn't hear about it on the news."

I saw it too and watched it glide northwest across the sky.

"Where?" Hazel cried, her neck craned skyward. "Where is it?"

I squatted behind her and pointed from her eye level. "See? It's moving."

She followed my finger. "I see it!" she enthused.

"Turn on the radio," Dad urged.

Mom ran in. The station was playing music. She left the radio on and came back out. We watched moments longer.

"Maybe they don't know," Dad said. "Helen, why don't you go call the station and tell them what we see."

I hesitated, then went. Mom helped me find the number in the phone book. I dialed. When a man answered, I said, "We're watching a satellite. Do you know whose it might be?"

There was a pause. "There are no satellites tonight," he said. "We always get the announcements when there is one, and we'll always keep our listeners informed. But there's no satellite tonight."

"But we've been watching it. It sure looks like a satellite."

"No. There's none tonight." The phone clicked.

I went back outside. "That was embarrassing," I said. "They didn't believe me."

We watched what surely looked like a satellite until it disappeared over the northwest horizon. I felt foolish.

The next morning Dad baled until the sun burned off the dew and he came in for breakfast. I still felt foolish for having called the radio station about a satellite that didn't exist.

As usual after the breakfast blessing, we turned on the radio to listen to the news. Just before the news, a reporter said, "We owe an apology to a young lady who called last night to tell us about a satellite."

We all stopped chewing and looked at the radio. "We told her there were none scheduled for that time," he continued. "And there weren't any scheduled. What we didn't know was that the USSR launched a satellite without announcing it. When we got the call, the unannounced satellite would have been visible in our skies. Our apologies, young lady, for not taking you seriously. You've got a good eye. If you see another satellite, please give us a call."

I could hardly believe my ears.

"Wow!" Dad said. "Do you feel better about that call now?"

"Yeah, I do. But you're the one who saw it," I said, pointing toward Dad.

"Yep," he said. "I *knew* it was a satellite!"

Satellites flying overhead weren't the only change that summer. It seemed strange without Frank and Emma to share in the fun and the work. It was great when they'd visit for a weekend.

On one of the weekends when Emma came, a young man at church seemed especially friendly with her . . . which probably accounted for the increase in her trips home.

In the barnyard, the calves started eating hay—it was a relief to be finished with bottle feeding. Dad milked the cow. Sometimes he milked the goats and fed the animals, sometimes I did. When it came to haying, he mowed the first couple rounds around a field—I was glad, because the mower sickle pushed out beyond the end of the mower just far enough that, if it got too close to the irrigation main line, it punched little holes in the pipe. That called for Dad to take time to make repairs. I did most of the raking. Dad did most of the baling. I drove the tractor while he pulled individual bales onto the slip, then stacked the hay. When one of the truckers who hauled alfalfa hay to a dairy in western Washington came to buy a load of hay, Dad helped load the truck.

In time, Dad turned the growing calves out of the barn into the pasture with the goats. The calves learned about electric fences the same way the sheep and goats had. I felt kind of sorry for them, but it was comical to see the expression on their faces as they bounced backward, then stared at the wire that shocked them.

"We've got to keep an eye on them," Dad said. "If cattle get into an alfalfa field, they can bloat."

"What's bloat?" I asked.

"If cattle eat a bunch of fresh alfalfa, they can get gas that fills their innards. They can swell so big that they can't breathe, so they die."

"But we feed them alfalfa all the time," I said.

"Dried alfalfa hay," Dad said. "They can eat the dry hay without any problem. But if they get into a green field, it can kill them."

Mom took over most of the chicken care. I still sanded eggs—my nickel wages had not increased. The fact that the number of eggs was decreasing was a mixed blessing—though it eased gathering, sanding, candling, weighing, and delivering the eggs into town, it was hard on the pocketbook.

One evening late in the summer at the supper table, I looked at Dad and asked, "Is the hay ready to cut again?"

Silence. He had a blank stare in his eyes. He looked like his mind must be off on some other subject. Then he jerked his head to the side. "What? What did you say?"

"Is the hay ready to cut?"

"Oh," he said. "Uh-h-h, I'll check it after supper."

Mom, Hazel, and I carried on a conversation.

Dad stared into space. A few minutes later, he said, "I've been thinking . . ."

What now? I thought. *Every time he starts out like that, there's some big change.*

Mom quit chewing, looked up, and fixed her eyes on Dad.

CHAPTER 37

What If . . .?

"We've worked hard," Dad said. "Everyone's worked hard. We've managed, but we sure don't have any extras. If we want a farm that's going to support us, we need to get more acreage into production."

Mom laid her fork down. I looked back and forth between the two. Was that fear in Mom's eyes? Was it fear in Dad's eyes?

"We're kinda between a rock and a hard spot," Dad finally said. "We're not going to improve our living unless we farm more land. We've got the land, but we don't have time to handle any more work."

Mom laid a hand on the back of Hazel's chair without taking her eyes off Dad's face. "I suspect you have some kind of an idea up your sleeve?"

"Yep, I do." Dad swallowed hard. "We've spent a lot of time carrying sprinkler pipes one by one across the fields. We don't have time to change anymore unless . . ."

Mom eyed Dad.

". . . unless we get wheel lines. If we'd break up some more ground and put in wheel lines, we could double our crops, maybe triple 'em."

"And the money?" Mom asked. "Where are we going to get the money?"

"That's the problem," Dad answered. "Money. We've tried to do this on a shoestring. And we're making progress, but it's so slow that, at this rate, I'll be in my grave before there's enough profit to make good use of the land. I think we'll have to ask for more help."

"What kind of help do you have in mind?"

"A loan. If we refinance the farm, next spring we could break sod on more acreage, put a couple wheel lines on it, and seed it."

Mom and Dad discussed it back and forth.

"So-o-o," I asked one day, "would we have more money for things we want?"

"Yes and no," Mom answered. "It might seem like we'd have more money, but we have to pay back the loan . . . plus interest on what we borrow. So, in a way, getting a bigger loan is like adding another bill we have to pay." She squinted like when she was thinking hard. "If we refinance," she added, "we'll have to be every bit as careful with money as we've ever been. Before we get a loan, we must be *positive* we can pay the money back."

The discussion continued off and on for weeks—the advantages, the disadvantages, the pros, the cons.

The calves had grown into sturdy young steers. Dad sold several at a cattle auction. When he got home, he handed the check to Mom—the family treasurer.

She looked at the amount and smiled. "That will definitely help pay the current bills."

Dad got a gleam in his eyes. "Think it was worth the trouble to feed calves?"

"Yeah," Mom said. "It was a good idea."

"Makes sense to me," Dad added, "to get calves next year too. They can eat our cull hay and I can take some to the auction any time."

"And we have the needed equipment now."

Dad chuckled. "Guess we're in the cattle business." Then his smile disappeared. "But raising a few calves isn't going to solve our bigger financial issues."

Talk of refinancing continued. Mom and Dad obviously researched it—the conversations began to include talk of interest rates with different loaning institutions. They finally made a decision to contact the Farm Home Administration (FHA).

That started a whole new discussion. At that point, FHA would not loan money to farmers who did not have reasonable living arrangements. Our shack—even with the great outdoors and granary for bedrooms—did not meet their requirements. If we were going to borrow money from them, we'd have to build a house. Yippee!

Which meant a bigger loan. Oh-h-h . . . not so good!

More discussion followed—more pros and cons. The advantages were obvious. The disadvantage—a loan hanging over the family finances. What if the wind took out new crops like they did at Uncle Max's place? What if a pump went out and we couldn't water young plants at a critical time? What if . . .? What if . . .? What if . . .?

The least we could do was draw house plans and see how much it would cost to build. We talked about what we'd want in our "big" house. Dad got out paper, pencil, and his trusty ruler and started drawing. He started with a simple rectangle and drew in a kitchen, a bathroom (with a real tub and toilet!), three bedrooms, and an open dining and living room area. He penciled in measurements.

Dad's final drawings showed a frame that was 28 by 37 feet. My proposed bedroom had nearly as much square footage as there was in our whole shack. Wow!

Would there be a basement? It would provide relatively inexpensive extra room, including a place to store produce and Mom's canned fruit and vegetables. It would provide cool space in the summer. A basement could also hold a furnace fueled by wood, paper, cardboard—basically anything that would burn.

What about the house walls? Should they be wood? "Concrete block would be safer if there ever was a fire," Dad said. "Block wouldn't be as stable in an area that had earthquakes, but there's more danger of fire than earthquakes here."

Mom and Dad decided they'd price building with the floor plan we'd discussed and Dad had drawn. In the plan they included an unfinished basement and simple concrete block walls.

They got contractor's bids. Mom and Dad filled out the application. The house plans met the FHA requirements. But, considering our income, would we be approved for a loan?

CHAPTER 38

Goals

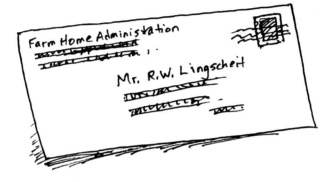

President Eisenhower started the new year off with a momentous event. There had been no new states admitted to the United States for 57 years—since 1912. But on January 3, 1959, the president signed a proclamation which admitted Alaska as the forty-ninth state. He also unveiled a new US flag with forty-nine stars.

All the talk about Alaska fueled family curiosity and conversations, but there were more urgent plans to consider—potential crops, digging a second sump, ordering new equipment, alterations to the house plan, and a wedding. Romance had bloomed, and Emma's letters and visits home included planning for her upcoming August wedding. She would move back home in midsummer and put wedding prep into high gear.

Someone eagerly checked the mailbox each afternoon. A letter from Emma or Grandma Miller was always a delight. Letters from Aunt Thelma kept us informed of what was happening with the cousins we missed. But that spring, we anxiously awaited mail from FHA. One afternoon when I checked for mail on the way home from school, a large, official-looking envelope from Farm Home Administration was one of the letters. I handed Mom the mail with that envelope on top. She took one look and headed out to the yard where Dad was repairing the rake—getting it ready for spring work. Hazel and I followed.

"We got some mail you may be interested in," Mom said.

Dad stood up and looked at the envelope. A smile and a frown got all mixed up on his face. "Well . . ." he said, "anyone want to know what our future holds?"

Mom stood there. I couldn't read her expression.

Dad pulled the pocketknife out of his pocket and sliced open the end of the envelope. He slid out a packet of papers and scanned down the first page. Tears threatened to brim. He smiled and choked out the words, "Our loan's approved!" He yanked the red handkerchief out of his overalls' back pocket and blew his nose. "It's approved," he said again. "We're going to have a busy summer!"

And so it was. As soon as the loan was approved, Dad found a disk at an implement dealer that was more suited to our sandy soil than the plow we had used to break sod before. The disk was nearly as wide as the tractor. "With more than a hundred acres to get ready to put into production," Dad said, "the disk will help get the job done a little faster."

I sighed. *More than a hundred acres?* I thought. I looked beyond the green, forty acres already producing. *This will take a while.*

As Mom and Dad discussed the future, Mom said, "Now that the hens are laying fewer eggs, I'm not sure they're worth the time and feed."

"Should I sell them?" Dad asked.

The conclusion of the discussion was the end of egg producing. Though that eased the workload, there was still plenty to do.

One afternoon after school, I rode along as Dad drove the tractor out to the new field. I stood on a floorboard, leaning against the fender. He made a few rounds around the new field. He explained about disking and showed me how to raise and lower the disk at corners. He demonstrated how, if he left the disk too deep in the soil, it could lug the tractor down. "Raise the disk up when the engine lugs," he said. "If you don't, the tractor will get stuck, and we'll have to dig it out."

Soon Dad stopped the tractor and crawled off. "Any questions?"

"Not yet."

"You'll do fine," he said. He turned and headed to the house.

I throttled up and let out the clutch. With the disk in the dirt behind me, I kept my right hand on the lever that would raise and lower the three-point-hitch with the disk attached. I let the front left wheel follow the rut between the disked sand and the virgin desert. Look front, look left, look behind, keep the tractor running smoothly, don't let it lug, lift the disk a whiff, lower it back down . . . At the corner, I cut the gas, lifted the disk, and stomped on the right brake. The tractor turned ninety degrees. I wrestled the steering wheel and got the left front wheel back in the rut the disk had left on the previous round.

All went well. I got more adept at making corners. Then I heard the engine lug down again, but didn't get the disk raised quickly enough. No matter what I did, the tractor wouldn't budge. I turned off the engine, crawled off the tractor, and started walking.

When I arrived at the farmstead, Dad was on his knees, working on the baler. He looked up. Before I said a word, he asked, "Get stuck?"

"Yeah," I said sheepishly.

He got up. "I'll get the shovel. Why don't you get a drink of water? I'll be right back."

We walked to the tractor. He dug out in front of the big, rear drive wheels and some in front of the disk. He started up the tractor, made sure the disk was lifted as high as it would go, then moved the tractor a few inches ahead, then a few more, and more. It was back on top, and I was in the disking business again.

After school let out for the summer, I got lots of disking practice.

I didn't have a watch, and the new field was farther from the house than those that already had crop growing. Dad put a pulley on a fifteen-foot pole. He attached a rope to the pulley and a white rag to the rope. He stood the pole on the field side of the poplar trees. (Those "sticks" Dad had planted had grown to probably twenty feet tall.) When Mom had dinner or supper ready, rather than having to come out to the field and wave me in, she ran the white flag up the pole. As mealtime approached—as determined by my body clock and growling stomach—I kept an eye out for the white flag flying in front of green poplar trees. I honored it by responding quickly to its invitation to food, then lowered it back down before returning to the field. (I didn't want to miss the next meal!)

Disking was a hot, dry, and dusty job. A bath and swim in the sump at the end of each day felt wonderfully cool and refreshing.

Day after day the sun managed to shine past the dirt that settled on me—my naturally light skin turned a tanned bronze.

I continued to disk. If Dad was home and saw me walking toward the shack, he'd get a shovel and head toward the field. As soon as the tractor was dug out, I proceeded around the square of diminishing size. I became more adept at learning just when I should raise the disk and when I could lower it. I got stuck less often.

As the challenge decreased, boredom increased. I belted out songs with varying enthusiasm, created poems in my mind, told stories to the sagebrush. One day when I heard the melodic trill of a meadowlark, I wondered, *Could I do that?*

"You've got plenty of time to try," I told myself. *Hm-m-m,* I thought. *I may not be able to play the piano very often, but I can practice meadowlark music as often as I want . . . for as long as I want.*

So I started trying to trill the fluted notes of the meadowlark song. Every time I spotted a meadowlark, I listened closely to its clear, piercing call. Then I whistled . . . and whistled. The first two notes came easily, but the trill was a tune of a different tone. Day after day, I watched for meadowlarks, each with its yellow breast with the black vee. When I spotted one, I listened carefully to each note it sang. I whistled . . . and practiced . . . and whistled some more as I drove up one side of the field, then down another.

When I saw and heard meadowlarks, I started singing back to them. I thought different ones looked a little perplexed. They usually flew away.

I didn't give up. I kept practicing. Trying to get the trill to work, I began flipping the end of my tongue in the middle of the snippet I practiced. It sounded better. I kept practicing.

A few days later a meadowlark sat on a sagebrush at the edge of the field and sang its cheerful song. I whistled my rendition. He answered. My mouth dropped open. I spit out the dust, then whistled again. He answered again. I haven't the slightest idea what we said, but we carried on a lengthy, melodic conversation before he flew away.

I felt ecstatic!

Eager to share the excitement, at dinner I told Mom and Hazel all about my practice and meadowlark conversation. I whistled my trill for them.

"Sounds like a bird," Hazel said.

I smiled. Even my little sister recognized my whistle as a bird call!

"Good job!" Mom enthused. After a moment she asked, "Do you realize what you've done these last few days?"

"What do you mean?"

Mom looked me straight in the eye. "You set a goal. That was good. You worked toward your goal. You worked with determination . . . until you accomplished it. That's fantastic!" She smiled and spoke her next words slowly and with emphasis. "If you can talk with meadowlarks, you can do anything you set your mind to . . . as long as you're willing to put in the work!"

CHAPTER 39

Dreams and Dread

I had to quit disking to mow hay on the planted fields, then rake. Dad baled on the days when he didn't work early at Glade Farms. When I wasn't busy harvesting hay, I went back to disking.

Dad ordered the main line and wheel lines that would be needed for irrigating the new fields. He and Mom hired a contractor to start building the house. Suddenly our quiet family farm turned into a beehive of activity. Stakes outlined the house. Contractors came and went. One showed up with a backhoe and dug the basement hole. The main contractor built forms for footings, floor, and walls. Concrete trucks came. Someone dug for and installed a septic tank and system. Progress seemed slow, but changes kept happening.

Emma worked at her job until mid-June, then came home to prepare for her August wedding. Sometimes she also changed sprinklers. The worst part for her was that she got stuck with the job of milking the cow again. I felt sorry for her—she rushed to milk before church, before wedding shopping trips to town, and before dates.

It wasn't just the rush to milk—there was the scent. She didn't always smell very good when she came in from leaning her head against Bossie's back quarters, from getting switched with the tail that had been who-knows-where, or from accidentally stepping in a fresh cow pie. And cleanup in the sump was a nuisance.

"Sure is nice to have someone else milking Old Boss!" Dad said one morning after he came in from baling. He grinned as he looked at Emma, "Sure you don't want to stay around and keep the job?"

Emma smirked and raised an eyebrow. "Positive!"

Dad sighed. "You're over eighteen," he said. "Guess we'll have to let you go."

Emma's fiancé visited often. Sometimes they went out on dates. Sometimes they visited right there on the farm.

Five-year-old Hazel loved to shadow them when they stayed. One evening, Emma's jolly friend noted a sparrow flitting nearby. He pointed to the bird. "Hazel, do you know how to catch a bird?"

"No. How?"

"If you put salt on a bird's tail, you can catch it," he said. "Go get a saltshaker from your mom."

Hazel ran to the shack. Mom played along and gave her a saltshaker. Hazel spent the evening trying to shake salt on various bird's tails. The couple had a quiet evening mostly to themselves.

As a twelve-year-old, I was excited that Emma would talk to me about her wedding plans. Not only that, she had asked me to be a bridesmaid and Hazel to be flower girl. She had purchased her wedding dress, but she planned to make Hazel's and my dresses and her veil. We brought Mom's old Singer treadle sewing machine from storage, squeezed it into the shack between the table and chests of drawers, and Emma sewed. After a swim in the sump, using the floating soap to wash off the sand and grit, I tried on my dress and Emma sewed and fitted some more. What fun to have a brand-new, pretty dress.

But that wasn't all there was to do. I kept up the disking. There was more action to watch in the fields too. Trucks brought main line pipes, sprinkler pipes, and metal half-wheels for the new fields. Workmen began at one end bolting the wheels together around the sprinkler pipes. Within a few days, two wheel lines stood at the edge of the field ready to use. Men from the power company put up poles and strung electric wires to the place where Dad had dug a new sump and where the new pump would go.

At the house, concrete cured, then block walls began to grow. Every evening when I came in from the field, I stopped to view changes on the house. Progress on the fields, the house, and wedding plans filled mealtime conversations.

Disking twenty-five acres with five-foot-wide swaths was a big job. And as soon as I got that patch done, there were three more just like it. What could I do to speed up the work? Ah, the corners.

Where the tractor turned and the disk was raised out of the dirt, a strip of raw land from each of the four corners toward the center of the field remained. Dad had said that after I finished the entire field, he would go disk those corner strips. Could I decrease their width? I could almost hear Mom's voice—"Whatever you do, always do your best." I pushed myself to time my actions perfectly so the strip of raw land would be narrower. The new challenge made disking more interesting.

It also caught Dad's attention. "Can't believe how narrow you're getting those corner strips," he said. "Good job."

Still, disking droned on, day after day. What new challenge could I come up with—besides watching for the food flag? Hm-m-m. Did I have to slow down so much at the corners?

Next corner, I didn't slow quite as much. It went fine. Next corner, I slowed less. I challenged myself further. Pretty soon I kept the throttle full bore as I approached the corner. At the same instant,

I lifted the disk and stomped on the right brake. The front tractor wheels rose off the ground. The large, right, rear, drive wheel, stopped, the left wheel kept turning. The front of the tractor swung right. I lifted my foot off the brake and lowered the disk. The left front wheel dropped into the rut and the tractor kept going.

That was fun.

A goal, a challenge, and more work well done!

When the new twenty-five-acre plot was disked and harrowed, Dad seeded it and we started watering with the wheel lines. That surely was easier than hand lines! I could start the engine with the rope pull and move the whole line by myself . . . in only minutes.

The established alfalfa field blossomed. We mowed, raked, baled, and stacked second cutting. Tiny green plants started showing in the newly planted field. I disked the patch next to it.

A couple weeks before Emma's wedding, a new thought crossed my mind. I shuddered. Nausea threatened to disgorge my breakfast. Since she had come home, Emma milked the cow every morning and every evening . . . no matter what else was going on. Dad had talked several times about how nice it was that he didn't have to stop everything else and milk. He'd gotten out of the habit, and he was enjoying that.

I'm the obvious next-in-line potential milker, I realized.

The thought pummeled me whether I was driving tractor, bathing in the sump, or trying to sleep. *Every morning,* I kept thinking, *seven days a week, before school, before church. Every evening, seven days a week, no matter how cold, no matter how hot, before parties, before meetings, before dates.*

My wedding enthusiasm dwindled. Dread took over my life.

Even though I had trouble focusing on anything other than my own dread, life went on in the nation. The news covered another proclamation. After fifty-seven years with forty-eight states, Alaska had been admitted on January 3, and on August 21, President Eisenhower signed a proclamation admitting Hawaii as the fiftieth state. Suddenly the forty-nine-star flag, introduced just eight months before, was out of date. But we'd have to wait before we saw a new fifty-star flag—wait for nearly a year.

Still busy disking and haying, the days for wedding prep counted down—fourteen, thirteen . . . seven, six . . . Each time Emma headed to the barn, I felt sick to my stomach. The closer the wedding date, the sicker I felt. Then I came up with a plan. I would be ready . . . right after the wedding. But would it work?

CHAPTER 40

Big House

Wedding day approached. Dresses were sewn, fitted, laundered, and ironed. Plans were set. Mom and Emma cooked up a storm all week to feed the wedding guests . . . and Emma milked.

Unfortunately, our house was not yet complete. Fortunately, it was closed in. Family we hadn't seen in months or years arrived, knowing they'd get to sleep in our new house before we did—on the floor. And have no running water, which meant using the outhouse.

The families of the bride and groom gathered for a picnic dinner Saturday at the park across the street from Franklin County Courthouse in Pasco. As the horde visited, enjoying both family's delicious offerings, Mom noticed a man sitting at a nearby picnic table, eyeing our heavily laden tables. "I'll bet he's hungry," she quietly told me.

The man looked like those we occasionally saw riding the nearby rails—long hair, long beard. It looked like it had been a long time since he'd seen a bathtub . . . or a swimming hole. It was so like Mom to notice someone in need.

She walked toward the man. My heart raced. *Is she safe?* I wondered.

Mom stepped up to the man. With sweet gentleness, she asked, "Would you like to join us for some lunch?"

The stranger's eyes sparkled an instant, then darkened as he looked around at the crowd. "Oh, no-o-o, Ma'am," he stammered. "I c-c-couldn't do that."

I felt puzzled by his response.

Mom smiled. "You'd be welcome."

He shook his head. "No."

"Are you hungry?" Mom asked. "Would you like me to bring you a plate of food?"

His eyes brightened again. "Yes, Ma'am. I'd love some!"

I felt sort of relieved for him.

Mom rounded a paper plate high with home-cooked food fit for a king—fresh-baked buns, potato salad, baked beans, homemade cookies, and more. She grabbed a napkin and plastic ware, then carried it all toward the man.

He stood as she approached, leaned forward in a slight bow. Mom held out the plate. He reached out to receive it. "Thank you, Ma'am. Thank you so-o-o much." He bowed again. "I am so-o-o hungry. Thank you. Thank you."

"There's more if you'd like."

"Oh, no, Ma'am. This will be plenty. Thank you so-o-o much."

He sat there and ate the whole plateful. Then he walked toward a garbage can and dropped the empty plate and disposable tableware into it. He looked up, caught Mom's eye, waved, and smiled.

Mom smiled and waved back.

Then the stranger turned and walked away.

He's really polite, I thought. *Maybe he's a good person just having a hard time right now.*

The conversation around me continued as I watched the man walk east toward the railroad tracks. Then a new thought struck like lightning. *Kind of like us. We've been having a hard time the last few years. We haven't had a real house. We've worked hard but, part of the time, the weather didn't cooperate. No matter the lack of money or convenience, it doesn't have to change who I am. I can be polite and kind no matter my circumstances.*

Maybe I should have applied the thought in the coming week.

Over the wedding weekend I enjoyed the family company, but delight diminished with every thought of . . . *milking.*

Emma's wedding was beautiful. I helped Mom clean up afterwards, and Dad had the milking done by the time we got home. *Yes!*

The next morning, I ate quickly. As soon as I finished, I jumped up and started clearing the table.

After Dad finished his breakfast, he went outside. Minutes later he came through the door, milk pail in hand. "Helen," he called, then spotted me enthusiastically washing dishes. "Oh-h-h," he muttered, "you're busy."

Dad stood there for a moment that felt like eternity. Out of the corner of my eye, I could see he was thinking. My heart pounded.

Then, without another word, Dad turned, pulled the door closed behind him, and disappeared. A little later he was back with a pail full of milk.

So far, so good! I thought. *But will it last?*

That afternoon I assisted Mom with canning peaches. Before milking time, I made it a point to be especially busy.

Somewhere in the middle of fifty quarts of the golden fruit—Dad's favorite—he again arrived with the milk bucket in hand. He glanced around. Likely saw the collection of processed jars, the six boxes of peaches waiting, the rows of full jars ready to be boiled, and the steam rising from the canner on the stove. He stood there for another eternal moment, then turned and went out to milk.

I tried to keep my sigh inaudible. I didn't dare let Mom in on my strategy.

The next morning, I ate quickly—even oatmeal couldn't sidetrack my scheme. As soon as I finished, I popped up to wash dishes.

After breakfast, Dad arrived with the milk pail . . . again. A lo-o-o-ong minute later he turned and went out, pail in hand.

Made it one more time! I sighed.

Evening—Dad milked again. Then another morning . . . evening . . . morning . . . evening . . . morning.

Occasionally I had second thoughts. *Am I being manipulative?*

Dad's dictums ruled, however, and I didn't know another way to get out of milking. Occasionally I wondered if milking might be a lot less work than everything I was doing to avoid it!

Repeatedly Dad came looking for me at milking time. Each time, I held my breath. Though I was regularly a good worker, Mom had probably never before had such eager and enthusiastic help . . . from anyone. Dad continued to carry the milk bucket away and milk Old Boss.

School started. Sometimes I raked hay before I left for school. But Dad kept doing morning milking! Sometimes I changed sprinklers or mowed hay after school. But Dad kept doing evening milking!

Will he keep it up? I wondered.

Each day we checked on house-building progress—electrical, plumbing. (Maybe someday we'd have running water and actually get to use the plumbing.) Hazel and I each got to pick the paint color and the pattern of flexible, thin, floor tiles for our own bedrooms. Sheetrock was added over the stud walls. We couldn't see from one end of the house to the other anymore. The rooms were painted. Each evening after the workers left, Hazel swept the scraps and dirt off the wood. Then floor tiles and light fixtures were added.

Finally, the last worker finished his job. We swept and mopped. The next day a neighbor helped move the kitchen range and refrigerator out of the shack and into the new house. We moved chests of drawers. We moved table and chairs into the dining area, Mom and Dad's bed into their bedroom, the double bed from the granary into my bedroom, and Hazel's and my single bed into her room. We moved food and dishes. Set a ten-gallon water can in the kitchen where water would be handy. We carried blankets and made beds.

Mom cooked supper in her new kitchen. We sat around the table with space to spare, no one accidentally kicking the next person. And soon we would move our things from Glade Farms. We would have the piano . . . and I could play it any time I wasn't working and no one was sleeping.

That night, I went to my bedroom. *My* bedroom. It was about the same square footage as the whole shack we'd moved out of that morning. And I had it all to myself. It was painted the pink I'd chosen. I twirled in delight.

That night I lay in bed in silence. With windows open, I listened for the whistle of the train. Because the windows were high on the wall, from my bed I saw two rectangles of black sky studded with stars. It felt so-o-o good to have a real house. To have a room to myself. To have the farm growing crops. I felt excited about the future.

I heard Mom's and Dad's voices quiet from the far end of the house. I heard Hazel's door creak open and barefoot steps pad down the hall. Then my little sister's voice, "Mama, it's too big. It's too lonely. Can we move back to the little house?"

1959 and Beyond

CHAPTER 41

Home

W e didn't move back to the shack. It became a toolshed again.

Hazel soon learned to appreciate more room—it probably helped that Mama Kitty could laze on the couch in the living room for a while some afternoons. Dad kept milking the cow. Mom enjoyed the expanded housing. Even though we couldn't afford piano lessons, I enjoyed practicing piano. Every month or two, after I had more-or-less learned another song, we'd go to a music store, I'd choose one song, and Mom would buy that sheet music for me.

Every now and again a steer or several broke out of the corral. When they did, they headed straight for an alfalfa field. When we spotted them, every other endeavor stopped.

On those days, we got major doses of exercise, running out and around the steers, easing them toward the corral, out and around again, back and forth. "Sure wish we had a dog like old Smokey," Dad said. "He could round up the cattle while we stood and watched."

Occasionally we lost a steer to bloat. Once, we lost several. As well as our hating to see any creature suffer, it was a severe blow to our finances.

In time, a puppy came to live with us. Stubby didn't have much of a tail to wag, but she was full of bounce and fun. She'd never take the place of Smokey, but she wormed her energetic self into our hearts. Stubby was smart and happy. She was part Australian shepherd, and herding came naturally.

One day when Stubby was still a pup, on our return from a trip to town, Dad declared, "Well, look at that!"

A big Holstein steer had escaped the corral. He probably had his eye on the alfalfa field. But Stubby had him safely cornered by the barn and corral.

"She's a keeper!" Dad exclaimed.

Even if our house was bigger, we still missed some conveniences. Water, for instance. The ever-present ten-gallon can was still with us. But there was room for it inside, so we never had to break ice before we could pour water. And when we finished washing dishes, we didn't have to carry the water out into the cold. All we had to do was pull the plug in the bottom of the sink. Such luxury!

A bucket of water stood by the toilet for flushing. In summer when we emptied the bucket, we went outside and refilled it at the garden irrigation faucet. In winter, we refilled it from the 500-gallon tank on the back of the truck. No one lost any sleep over the outhouse feeling lonely.

And no more jaunts outside in the heat or the cold to brush teeth. Yes, we still had to take our cupful of water with us to the bathroom sink, but it was a great improvement.

Baths? In summer, the sump still provided for swimming and bathing. In cold weather, even if we did have to heat water in the canning kettle and carry it into the bathroom, it was a privilege to be able to stretch out in a real bathtub. All we had to do for privacy was close the door. And none of us had to hang out in the frigid wind, rain, or snow while someone else bathed.

A few years later, we hired a well driller and got to retire the five-gallon and ten-gallon cans we had used for hauling drinking water.

Was everything easy? No! The wind still blew. New neighbors moved in a mile west of us and plowed and planted. We caught the drift of their blowing sand.

We still worked hard. Dad repaired old equipment rather than buy new. Mom scrimped and saved so we could pay off the farm loan.

We disked new fields and were pelted by our own sandstorms. We tried a variety of crops, but turned back to alfalfa. We planted it, then, cutting after cutting, irrigated, mowed, raked, baled, stacked, and sold it or fed it to a growing herd of steers—a big part of the farm savings account. Finances eased as crops multiplied.

Christmas 1959, the package with my name was about the size of a stationery box, it weighed little more than a few feathers. When I shook it, odd noises surprised me.

On Christmas Eve I opened the package to discover a clothespin, a marble, and a couple coins. A piece of paper lay in the bottom of the box—a note: "Good for one new dress at J. C. Penney's."

"A new dress?" I exclaimed. "At a store?"

The day after Christmas, Mom and I went to town to take advantage of the sales. We climbed wide stairs in the center of the store to the girls' and women's department. Shocked, I looked from one rack of dresses to another. So-o-o many!

We carried an armload of dresses to the fitting room. Mom patiently let me decide. We probably set a record that day for the longest-held dressing room.

Eventually I chose a blue plaid dress with a white collar. Mom paid, the clerk folded *my* dress carefully and slid it into a paper bag. She smiled as she handed it to me.

A brand-new dress! I smiled as I descended the stairs and skipped to the pickup.

I wore that special dress for my eighth-grade picture. I loved it until it was threadbare.

Years later, I worked my way through college by coming home every summer to drive equipment, change sprinklers, feed animals, and do whatever else needed to be done inside or outside.

More years later, I learned by accident that, although I had tried to sing very quietly when I raked hay at three or four in the morning, someone had heard me—our neighbor's dog. Not sure if Barney liked my music or not, but he accompanied my singing . . . with howling . . . which kept our neighbor, who'd just arrived home from the bar, wide awake until I quit singing. Oops!

As for zucchini, now I grow it in my own garden and enjoy it. Oatmeal? I eat it—without urging. Camping? My husband and I enjoy camping, but I do appreciate coming home to running water!

To this day, I have never milked a cow. Decades after I conspired to avoid milking, Dad lived in an assisted living facility. We visited as best we could, given his advanced Parkinson's disease. One summer afternoon as we sat in a swing in the backyard gazebo, I talked about farm memories. Dad grinned—his heart still lived on the land. Then I told him about my enthusiastic helpfulness after Emma's wedding . . . for the express purpose of avoiding milking. He chuckled. His eyes sparkled. He patted my knee and slurred, "But you did everything else!"

The years slipped by. Our family had finally moved into the big house (which wasn't really very big). But success wasn't found in bigger walls. The house was finally surrounded by flourishing fields. But success wasn't in the fields, the haystacks, or the corrals full of cattle.

Success came day by day as we kids grew—not just in stature, but also in character. Success came as imperfect parents sought to train imperfect kids to live with integrity. Success came as we learned to work, to play, to plan, to recognize that things can be important, but people are invaluable. Success came as we grew tough enough to conquer in spite of loss, but tender enough to hurt with the hurting. None of us are famous, all of us are successful. None of us are wealthy, all of us have enough to care for ourselves and to share with others.

Success came as the little things of our early years impacted the future. For instance, the box of food that showed up on our porch during a year when we—and many surrounding farmers—were just trying to survive. Because of that gift, we understand the delight and hope a simple bit of kindness can bring. As adults, different ones of us have sleuthed until we found real need. Boxes of groceries have been left on others' porches, vehicle repair costs have been covered, utility bills have been paid. Volunteer stints in impoverished countries have helped build churches and schools. Christmas parties for a special purpose have been hosted—each participant brought a gift to be donated to a local shelter that helps those willing to leave behind addictions and change the course of their lives.

We've received. Now we have the delight of giving . . . an especially poignant pleasure when it can be anonymous.

Some kind soul who put that box on our doorstep years ago probably expected to help one family for a few days. Instead, they touched a world for decades. And the kindness ripples on.

Success came as Mom and Dad grew a life they both loved. Mom was able to stay just where she wanted—on the farm—until her last breath. Because of failing health, Dad needed to move into assisted living. He hated to leave. "I just can't get the dirt out of my veins," he said. Both Mom and Dad loved the land. Family members still own and treasure the farm . . . as well as the memories.

We kids learned later that we were poor. But thinking back, I realize we weren't poor—we just didn't have much money. Though it wasn't always what we wanted to eat, we never went hungry. Though it wasn't always what we wanted to do, we always had something to do. We had parents who cared enough to laugh when we were funny and discipline when they thought we needed it. (We kids didn't always agree with them on the latter.) We were rich in things that mattered.

We all survived the sand. Like alfalfa roots, our family bonds grew deep. The tough times, stirred together with old-fashioned values, made us strong.

Now I remember our earlier home in the woods with fondness, but when I think of "home," I think of a farm in the desert where the sun shines, the wind still blows sand and cools the air, and, if you look hard enough, you can see past mountains of struggles to a future where you can harvest rewards forever. When I think of "home," I think of my family working together, worshipping together, playing together.

Yes, we watered the sand with sweat and tears. At times, Dad's dream felt like a nightmare. But through the tough years, through all the headaches and heartaches, together Mom and Dad led their brood in learning a dream is worth working for, holding onto hope means putting your whole heart into reaching its goal, and "hard" does *not* mean impossible.

EPILOGUE

And Now?

On the farm, pivot irrigation systems, also known as circles, replaced hand lines and wheel lines. A swather retired the mower and rake. A harrow bed eased getting the hay out of the field and stacking it. Family members still own and love the farm.

And the kids who survived the shack and the sand? We all grew up and married.

Emma later used the quiet determination she'd perfected while surviving her brother's never-ending mischief—she went back to school when she was a mom with four rambunctious little kids and became a nurse. She spent years giving her heart and skills to people in hospitals and ambulances and, now, to grandchildren and great-grandchildren.

Frank has been a successful entrepreneur and a drilling supervisor with major companies, responsible for drilling footings for projects such as freeway overpasses, tunnels, and Columbia River dams. He has three children and is delighting in grandchildren and great-grandchildren. He still teases and guarantees, with a grin, that he totally deserved every bit of grief his sisters returned to him.

Helen became a nurse, author, and inspirational speaker. To be heard, she no longer needs to visualize sheep and goats in the back of the room. She loves teaching classes that help ordinary people write stories that inspire and has enjoyed volunteering in various countries. Even on tough days, she considers herself "Blessed."

Hazel, the baby, loves being a grandmother. After college, she raised two children and assisted hundreds of others as the US-based office manager for a nonprofit organization with schools and an orphanage in Bangladesh. She lives on and manages the farm. She delights in the learning and exploits of her grandchildren. Except for brief camping trips, she no longer has any desire to move back to a "little house."

And the whole bunch of us all love and respect each other.

Historical Setting

Today you can drive for hours through eastern Washington state and see productive cropland, vineyards, and orchards. Fruitful green covers 670,000 acres. In 2014, according to the US Bureau of Reclamation, the Columbia Basin Project provided over a billion dollars in power generated and $1.27 billion in irrigated crops (that's "B" as in billion—$1,270,000,000). Agriculture and processing its crops form the basis of the area's economy.

But how did the desert come to bloom? How did it become a breadbasket to the world?

The American West

After the Homestead Act of 1862, pioneer families flocked west with dreams of fertile farms, only to have their hopes dashed—large tracts of the western half of the nation were arid. Because of lack of water for crops, animals, and people, many settlers gave up and left. Others tried various irrigation systems—water wheels, pumps, or hauling water to farms some distance from the limited rivers and streams. Private and state-sponsored irrigation ventures often failed due to lack of funds and/or engineering skills.

Pressure mounted for the federal government to become involved in reclaiming the land—soon called "reclamation." As early as 1866, the United States Congress passed an act granting right-of-way over public lands for irrigation ditches. In 1888, Congress appropriated funds to the United States Geological Survey to study the potential for irrigation in the arid areas of the West. Other legislation followed. In 1900, both Democratic and Republican platforms contained pro-irrigation planks. In 1902, a reclamation act passed Congress and was signed by President Theodore Roosevelt. The original act included sixteen states, including Washington. In 1906, Texas was added.

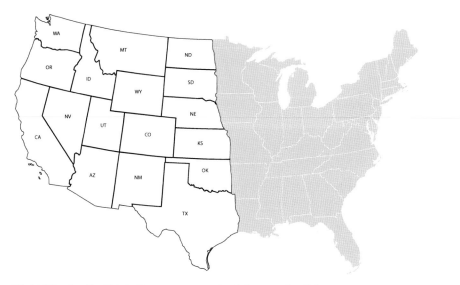

"Arid West"—By 1906, Congress recognized that much of these seventeen western states needed irrigation if the land was going to support settlers.

By 1907, twenty-four reclamation projects had been authorized. Though eastern Washington's need was recognized in the original act, no irrigation project was approved for that area.

Columbia Basin

In 1918, a visionary Wenatchee, Washington, newspaper editor began publishing articles touting the construction of a Columbia River dam about ninety miles northwest of Spokane. After much opposition, the dam was eventually approved. With the country reeling from the Depression, construction began in 1933, promising employment, as well as hydropower and irrigation water.

Grand Coulee Dam became the largest concrete structure ever built. At 550 feet tall and 5,223 feet wide (only 57 feet short of a mile), it required nearly 12 million cubic yards of concrete—seen by some as enough concrete to build a highway from Seattle, Washington, to Miami, Florida. (Although it remains the largest dam in the United States, the Three Gorges Dam in China, completed in 2009, surpassed the size of the Grand Coulee Dam.)

Grand Coulee Dam's first generator began producing power in 1941, the same year the United States entered World War II. While the war raged, irrigation waited. The dam's electricity provided power to the region's aircraft and aluminum industries and to the army's nuclear facility at Hanford.

After the war, construction of hundreds of miles of canals for irrigation finally began. The first irrigation water from Grand Coulee Dam arrived at potential farms in 1952.

The 1950s

After World War II, the Cold War grew between the United States and the USSR (Union of Soviet Socialist Republics). Would capitalism or communism win? The war of words and espionage born of distrust led to nuclear weapons, intercontinental ballistic missiles, and a space race.

At home, the United States experienced a baby boom and an economic boom. With continued expansion of military power, citizens seemed confident in a future of peace and prosperity. Manufacturing of nonmilitary items increased, creating more and more products to meet the needs and desires of growing families. Unemployment and inflation were low; wages were higher than they'd ever been. The middle class had more money to spend. Cars became affordable and common. Suburbs with modest, inexpensive tract houses grew up around cities, and more families were able to own their own homes.

Televisions also became common and included programs that sought to entertain while reinforcing values such as patriotism, faith, family, and conformity to society's norms. For instance, culture and media urged women to embrace traditional gender roles—to stay home and take care of their husbands and children, to allow their husbands to play the dominant role in their families.

Not everyone experienced the boon of the 1950s in equal proportion. The blight of segregation began to be recognized, and the Civil Rights Movement was born. Families with low income still struggled.

In the 1950s, while much of the country prospered and lived

comfortably, a variety of farmers moved to the Columbia Basin in eastern Washington with dreams of fertile fields, happy families, and independence in the postwar boom.

Our Family

After World War II had ended in 1945, Dad, two brothers-in-law, and their wives saw opportunity in the building and baby booms occurring in the United States—they formed "3 in 1 Lumber Company" near Willamina, Oregon. They built a small, portable sawmill. Not only could they move the sawmill from one logging site to another, but they could also saw logs into various dimensions of rough-cut lumber—2 x 8, 2 x 4, 1 x 4, etc. This meant they could utilize most of each log, leaving the least possible waste.

Their sawmill in the mountains on the east side of Oregon's Coast range supported a thriving community consisting of the three families and a number of employees. The rural school and church encouraged further growth. When the sun shone on the Gilbert Creek community on a day off work and school, the aunts, uncles, cousins, and friends enjoyed hikes in the wooded hills, softball games, and trips over the mountains to the beach—generally, with a picnic. If it rained, no worries—the mill had supplied lumber to build a large gymnasium. It provided ample space for games like dare base, snap the whip, and volleyball. Or riding bikes up and down boards placed against the rostrum. With creative kids (and adults), there was no limit to the fun.

Dad, however, sometimes complained of back and leg pain. A doctor told him he should move to a drier climate, that if he didn't quit slogging in the mud of the rain-soaked hills, he would experience increasing pain as the years passed. That advice reignited a dream Dad had nursed since his teen years while living with his grandparents on their farm. Dad told us stories about the abundant crops his grandfather grew in the flatlands of southeastern Idaho. He dreamed about farming. But how could he change things?

Business boomed at the sawmill . . . until 1950. Then timber supply diminished—much of the timber in the area was under contract to larger lumber companies. The small 3 in 1 Lumber Company

In the comfortable Oregon house—before the nightmare opportunity. Pictured from left to right: Frank, Dad, Helen, Mom, and (in the back) Emma. Hazel is yet to be born.

finally found timber nearly two hundred miles south near Bandon, Oregon. That fall, the two-room schoolhouse at Gilbert Creek, instead of being divided by grades 1–4 and 5–8, was divided by those whose families were moving to Bandon and those whose families were staying at Gilbert Creek.

All our cousins on Mom's side of the family were among those moving. Our immediate family bid them goodbye and stayed in Gilbert Creek.

At first, Dad drove to Bandon early on Sunday mornings for the work week, then returned home on Thursday nights. Eventually that stopped. Dad occasionally felled a load of logs and sold them to a local mill.

Then came 1954. An "opportunity" arose . . . and an announcement that would turn our comfortable family life upside down.

Surviving the Sand

In the early 1950s, much of the Columbia Basin was still desert—think sagebrush, sandburs, horned toads, scorpions, rattlesnakes. Grateful for irrigation, new pioneers broke sod. At first, many lived in shacks or tents while they looked forward to bountiful harvests to supply money for building adequate housing. These farmers arrived with varying assets, varying motivation, and varying knowledge of farming. They soon discovered that none of the roads were named Easy Street.

Sandstorms slashed young crops' leaves and buried many farmers' dreams. Some settlers stayed till they used up their assets, then moved back to previous endeavors or moved on to new enterprises. Some planted their family roots deep in their dreams . . . and in their sand.

The family of R. W. (Wayne) and Gladys Lingscheit, whose story is told in this book, is just one of those families who stayed. With grit, they and many other farmers survived tough times and transformed desert into fields that feed the world

Special Thanks

Many individuals helped birth this book. I greatly appreciate each contribution, little or large. Special thanks to each one, including the following:

- My brother and sisters—Frank, Emma, and Hazel. They shared memories, answered questions, read reams of manuscript pages, gave suggestions, shared photographs, and answered *more* questions with utmost patience and interest in the project.
- Cousins who filled in details and gave enthusiastic support.
- Neighbors then and neighbors still—Ernie Petty and Floyd and Jeannine Ossman. They also answered many questions, clarified details, and verified that hardship was an experience shared by the early farming community.
- Franklin County Historical Society & Museum who answered questions, shared resources, and suggested I contact Washington State University Press.
- Franklin County Public Works Department who helped with road information.
- Bureau of Reclamation representatives who answered still more questions and verified facts.
- The members of my writing critique group who helped strengthen the experience of readers.
- Readers of the manuscript who made valuable suggestions.
- Editor Linda Bathgate and her crew at WSU Press who encouraged me with their suggestions, demonstrated utmost patience with my questions, and brought this project to fruition.

- Illustrator Caryn Lawton, who stepped up to provide illustrations that bring words to life and a cover that accurately encapsulates the barrenness of a tough and stormy start.

Thank you, each one, for helping to preserve history!